SINGAPORE
PERSPECTIVES
2009
The Heart of the Matter

SINGAPORE
PERSPECTIVES
2009
The Heart of the Matter

Edited by

Tan Tarn How

Published by

World Scientific Publishing Co. Pte. Ltd.

5 Toh Tuck Link, Singapore 596224

USA office: 27 Warren Street, Suite 401-402, Hackensack, NJ 07601

UK office: 57 Shelton Street, Covent Garden, London WC2H 9HE

British Library Cataloguing-in-Publication Data
A catalogue record for this book is available from the British Library.

SINGAPORE PERSPECTIVES 2009: THE HEART OF THE MATTER

ISBN-13 978-981-4280-62-4 (pbk)
ISBN-10 981-4280-62-3 (pbk)

Printed in Singapore.

Contents

Contents

Foreword

Singapore Perspectives is a flagship event of the Institute of Policy Studies (IPS). Through the years, it has achieved a good standing and has a good following as the conference systematically addresses issues of significance to Singapore's society and its future.

In organising Singapore Perspectives 2009, the IPS team decided to build on the theme of the 2008 Conference, that is, the future of Singapore, and pull together the various threads of "heartware" and economic concerns. Hence, we posed the four questions of the rising cost of living and doing business in Singapore, the rootedness of Singaporeans, sustaining Singapore's hub role, and the engagement of citizens in national development.

The four questions we chose to address are inter-related fundamental issues. With this focus on "The Heart of The Matter", we anticipated interesting ideas and recommendations. Such "remedies", though they may not be conclusive or even immediate, would in turn play an important role in shaping future policy planning in Singapore.

The dialogue should enliven public discourse and enrich Singaporeans' understanding of the dynamics which characterise our society. An active exchange and reflection to create a better tomorrow helps to strengthen the openness of one's mind and clarity, clarity of thoughts and to maintain the balance of individual perspectives and community attitudes.

Singapore is a unique multiracial society, geographically small but mentally big, driven by a constant sense of security and a passionate "can-do" spirit. The governance is exceptional and its paradigm has not been seen elsewhere. We need to enlarge our mindshare on how to go forward in an effective manner so that we preserve what has been accomplished as we manage the changes around us.

Ambassador Ong Keng Yong

Director, Institute of Policy Studies,
Lee Kuan Yew School of Public Policy,
National University of Singapore

Acknowledgements

The Institute of Policy Studies is grateful to the following donors for their support of the Singapore Perspectives 2009 Conference held on 19 January 2009.

Principal Donors

TEMASEK
HOLDINGS

Donors

Editor's Acknowledgements

I wish to thank my research assistant Tan Simin for her invaluable help in copy-editing the chapters with me and managing administrative details of preparing the manuscript for publication. I also wish to thank my IPS colleagues for getting some of the chapters ready: Senior Research Fellow Gillian Koh, Research Fellow Leong Chan Hoong, and Research Assistants Chua Chun Ser and Debbie Soon.

Tan Tarn How

The Big Picture

Singapore Perspectives 2009: The Heart of the Matter

19 JANUARY 2009, SHANGRI-LA HOTEL
Chairman's Opening Address
TOMMY KOH

SALUTATION

Mr Lee Tzu Yang, Ambassador Ong Keng Yong, Your Excellencies, friends and members of the IPS family. A very warm welcome to Singapore Perspectives 2009. Since we are at the start of the new Gregorian year and a week from the new Lunar New Year, I would like, on behalf of the IPS family, to wish all of you good luck in this challenging year. To those of you who are employees, I hope that your jobs will not be affected. To those of you who run businesses, big and small, I wish you success in your plans to restructure, to reduce cost, to increase productivity and to seize new opportunities in the midst of adversity. And to all of you, I wish you good health, peace and success in the New Year.

FEAR OF DECLINING SUPPORT FOR NON-PROFIT SECTOR

One of the consequences of the economic downturn is the likely decline in support for philanthropy. This is to be expected. However, on behalf of the non-profit sector of Singapore, I would like to make an appeal to our profitable corporations, foundations whose endowments have not suffered a major hit, and high net-worth individuals not to reduce their generosity in the year ahead. In this regard, I would like to thank the 18 sponsors of this conference. Our three principal sponsors are: Keppel Corporation, the Standard Chartered Bank and Temasek Holdings. The other 15 sponsors, in alphabetical order are: Hill & Knowlton, Housing & Development Board, Jardine Cycle & Carriage Limited, Maritime and Port Authority of Singapore, Nanyang Polytechnic, Nanyang Technological University, National University of Singapore, Ngee Ann Polytechnic, Philips Electronics Singapore Pte Ltd, Republic Polytechnic, Shell Companies in Singapore, Singapore Management University, Singapore Polytechnic, SMRT Corporation and Temasek Polytechnic. I thank Chang Li Lin for securing the 18 sponsors.

Please join me in giving our 18 sponsors a big round of applause.

This is the first Perspectives organised under our new Director, Ambassador Ong Keng Yong. The person in charge of the intellectual content is Dr Yap Mui Teng. The persons in charge of everything else are Irene Lim and Catherine Lim. Please join me in congratulating Keng Yong, Mui Teng, Irene and Catherine for doing an outstanding job in conceptualising and organising this year's Perspectives.

THE HEART OF THE MATTER

The sub-title of this year's conference is: "The Heart of the Matter". What does it mean? I think Keng Yong and Mui Teng want us to think about four fundamental questions facing Singapore. What are they? First, can Singapore afford a high cost Singapore? Second, can Singaporeans remain rooted? Third, can Singapore preserve its hub status? Fourth, can the government do less and the people do more? In order not to pre-empt the discussions, I have followed my wife's advice to hold my tongue and not to share with you my views on those four questions. I promise, however, to participate actively in the discussions at the different sessions.

THE BIG PICTURE

We live in a highly globalised world. Singapore has consistently been ranked No. 1 or No. 2 in the A.T. Kearney/Foreign Policy Globalization Index. Singapore is also a very small and open economy and society. Almost nothing which happens here is unaffected by developments outside Singapore. We also live in a highly competitive world. It is desirable for us to learn from the lessons and best practices of other cities and countries. In order to give us that big picture, we have invited Mr Peter Ong, the Managing Partner for Gallup, in Singapore, Hong Kong and Southeast Asia, to speak to us.

ELECTRONIC POLL

There are over 600 participants at this conference. It is not possible, given the time constraint, for every one of you to express your views orally. We have, therefore, decided to introduce the electronic polling of your opinions to the four questions at the end of each session. We hope that all of you will participate and give us the benefit of your views.

Thank you very much and have a great day.

CHAPTER 1

Forging New Paths with Audacity and Vision

PETER ONG

In this talk, I will provide you with my best visualisation of Singapore now and in the years to come, and my thoughts on the issues which are at the heart of the matter.

NEW PARADIGM NEEDED: FOLLOWING FOOTSTEPS TO FORGING PATHS

First off, I will discuss where Singapore is today. From 1965 to 2009, Singapore underwent a remarkable transformation, from the initial steps of nation building to our push to be a "Global City of Distinction" and the "Best Home for All". We have done very well. The smarts, dedication and hard work of our political and public service leaders and the aligned and joint efforts of our business enterprises and citizens have all helped Singapore achieve much success in this short period. Although geographically Singapore is and always will be a little red dot, we have punched above our weight. Nowadays, Singapore is considered a "giant" in the world economy. Talented people of all nationalities are flocking here and we have evolved into a cosmopolitan city of world-class standards. Recent events bear strong testimony to Singapore's place in the world: it was to Temasek Holdings and the Government of Singapore Investment Corporation (GIC) that world-class companies came a-calling for assistance during the present financial crisis.

As we move towards 2015, when we will be (gasp) half a century old, there will be fewer footsteps of great countries and cities for us to follow, and there will be fewer blueprints of success that we can rely on, to "rapidly copy and smartly improve upon". Moving forward, Singapore can no longer afford to "follow the footsteps of others". Rather, we must embrace new ways of thinking and seeing the world, and bravely and confidently forge new paths ahead. This is one of the roles and responsibilities of well-respected, well-regarded First World countries, and we in Singapore must play our part. We must forge new paths at a strong clip to catch up with established cities like New York, London, and San Francisco; and we must ensure that we stay (way) ahead of rapidly emerging cities in Asia like Shanghai, Beijing, Mumbai and Bangalore. Other than competing on a city-by-city basis, retaining our position of strength amongst the other Asian Tiger economies of Hong Kong, Taiwan and South Korea remains part of the game.

Forty-four years post-independence, Singapore is at the forefront of the First World. By many established yardsticks of success, we have indeed arrived. The questions we need to ask today: "How can we sustain our success?" and "How can we get better?"

NEW FLYING INSTRUMENTS REQUIRED:
THE X-RAY AND THE MRI

Albert Einstein once said: "We cannot solve problems by using the same kind of thinking we used when we created them." Singapore is exactly at this juncture. To forge new paths, we need new tools, new dashboards, new visualisations, new methods, improved insights, and an enhanced way of alignment and collaboration across government ministries, statutory boards, associated agencies, private enterprises, citizens and Permanent Residents. Just as the scanning by MRI (magnetic resonance imaging) was a vast improvement over the X-ray in the field of medical imaging, and that both of them are very much needed in healthcare today, we need to keep the best of the old and complement that with the new and improved. Over the next few minutes, I will share with you some frameworks and visualisations which I believe will be helpful in facilitating Singapore to further improve and achieve.

First off, let us talk about the power of leading indicators. Leading indicators are metrics that allow policy makers and business leaders to anticipate and predict the future, and thereafter to take smart moves and wise steps to create the most positive and meaningful future possible. Here is an interesting story on leading indicators. In May 2007, when Gallup Chairman & CEO Jim Clifton and I were preparing for a series of senior political leader meetings in Singapore, we looked at data and patterns from the United States. And one of the interesting things we saw, from Gallup's Daily Poll in America, was that Americans were saying that they did not have as much "spare change" as they would like to get on with their lives, to spend it on things which they enjoy and which bring them happiness. Also, the number of Americans who said that they worried about money, that they sometimes struggled to put food on the table and a shelter above their families' heads, was increasing. These patterns and insights surprised Jim and I as America appeared to be doing rather well at that time. We then looked at data across large American companies. And we were struck by what we saw was happening at huge companies like Wal-Mart. Wal-Mart was cancelling and postponing large orders from low-cost countries like China. What was happening?

When Jim and I met up with the senior political leaders in Singapore in June 2007, we openly shared the insights and visualisations that we saw, and admitted that we did not have all the answers. But we told them that the writing was on the wall. Something rather large and very bad is looming in the distance in America, the economy was starting to slow rather dramatically and that people on Main Street and companies on Wall Street were seeing and feeling it, and the growing problem was being reflected in the behaviours, feelings, thoughts and actions of Americans and American corporations as captured by Gallup's Daily Poll in America. Fast forward to today. We all know what happened next. Wall Street, the sub-prime crisis, and the economy of America tanked... ... and took the whole world along with it. We are in the midst of this global downturn, and people all across the world, including many Singaporeans, are hurting. Wal-Mart postponing and cancelling large orders: that is a leading indicator of the extent of the downturn. Greater numbers of Americans not having "spare change", or the personal economics to get around, struggling to put food on the table and a roof over their family's heads, these are also leading indicators.

9

Leading indicators are essential and necessary to anticipate and predict the future way in advance such that the right steps can be taken, early and proactively. Leveraged well, leading indicators will allow us to see in the horizon, all sorts of swans, white or black.

Forging new paths as we move forward rather than simply following footsteps will necessitate that Singapore's leaders jointly gaze at a crystal ball of leading indicators, such that multiple ministries, statutory boards and agencies can all take aligned and oftentimes complex steps and actions way in advance to influence Singapore and Singaporeans, such that a better future can be created. Doing so will allow Singapore to navigate the waters ahead as best as we can. Leading indicators strategically and smartly analysed will facilitate sense-making, decision-making, policy-making and the most important of all, future-making. Leading indicators will allow Singapore and Singaporeans to forge new paths ahead, especially when the vista is not all that clear.

Table 1 Singapore ranks highly on a number of indices, and not so highly on others

How Singapore Stands

Where Singapore is Top	Singapore's Score
Law & Order Index	97
National institutions Index	87
Youth Development Index	92
Food & Shelter Index	98
Community Basics Index	91
Personal Health Index	90

Where Singapore Needs Improvement	Singapore's Score
Work Index	44
Personal Economics Index	67
Positive Experience Index	64
Thriving Index	49
Diversity Index	61
Optimism Index	62

Gallup surveys 140 countries every year on 100 core questions. We know what 98 percent of the world's population is thinking, feeling, and what their opinions, pain and happy points are. Singapore stands at the absolute top, whether compared as a country or as a city, on six of Gallup's indices (See Table 1):

- Law & Order
- National Institutions
- Youth Development
- Food & Shelter
- Community Basics
- Personal Health

These are areas where Singapore's value proposition is at its strongest. Many of them are the reasons that businesses and talents relocate their headquarters here and why citizens and PRs are so satisfied with Singapore as a place to live, work and play. Satisfaction for a country or city can often be attained through strong national, financial and community infrastructure, especially when there is an absence in its citizens and PRs of negative feelings like sadness, pain, suffering and depression. Singapore excels in these areas. On the other hand, engagement for a country or city necessitates the presence of positive feelings like optimism, hope, efficacy, laughter, a full arrestment of the senses, *et cetera*, in addition to the absence of negative feelings. This is where Singapore needs to improve. Helping Singaporeans find a job which they enjoy and which best utilises their talents other than just finding a job *per se*, increasing their hope and optimism levels and the number of positive experiences they encounter, inculcating the belief that they are thriving rather than just surviving, *et cetera*, these are areas which I believe Singapore seriously needs to focus on, so as to propel itself to the forefront of the First World. If we can nail these areas where we are already in the top one-third of all countries polled by Gallup, Singapore will be second to none, where businesses and talents, foreign or home-grown, will find most engaging to live, work, play, and more importantly, achieve.

BUSINESS CONCEPTS EXTENDED: POPULATION SEGMENTS, ENGAGED CITIZENS AND CRM

In business speak, we talk about "Customer Segments", "Engaged Customers" and "CRM", or Customer Relationship Management. Many a Chairman, CEO and CFO knows and believes strongly that customers are the lifeblood of any organisation, and that the more the enterprise does to strongly engage and retain them, the better their business, revenue and profits will be. If we are to extend these very important and very useful business concepts to Singapore, we will be able to better improve and impact the lives of Singaporeans. Let me explain what I mean. Other than simply thinking about Singapore as a country or a city, we can think of Singapore in terms of "Population Segments" very much like "Customer Segments", "Engaged Citizens" very much like "Engaged Customers" and "Citizen Relationship Management" rather than "Customer Relationship Management". Think about how powerful such a visualisation will be. If our policy makers, political and public sector leaders are to leverage these new concepts and see Singapore as made up of various citizen segments, all waiting, wanting and needing to be tightly engaged, and embrace and embark on Citizen Relationship Management initiatives, we will all be able to move one step closer to building engaged Singaporeans whose hearts, minds, thoughts and actions are all for, and about Singapore.

Chart 1   Citizen engagement is built on several components, with each component being represented by one to two statements

Citizen Engagement

Increased Community, City and Country Commitment & Effectiveness

Passion	**Singapore is irreplaceable to me.** **I feel passionate about Singapore.**
Pride	**I am proud of Singapore.** **Singapore is part of who I am.**
Integrity	**When I have a problem,** **Singapore always treats me fairly.**
Confidence	**I can safely assume that Singapore** **will always keep its promises to me.**
Rational Foundation	**Singapore fulfills my basic** **expectations.**

As Singapore is already operating in the First World, many of our citizens' basic expectations of what a country and a city should provide have already been met. What does this mean? This means that in the Citizen Engagement hierarchy, both the Confidence and Integrity components as well as the Rational Foundation component are well-met and well-achieved (See Chart 1). It is in the higher-order areas of Pride and Passion where Singapore's leaders need to turbocharge improvement. We need to come up with new ideas and implement new steps to create, build and sustain the Pride and Passion of Singaporeans about Singapore. We need Singaporeans to say the following:

- I am proud of Singapore.
- Singapore is part of who I am.
- Singapore is irreplaceable to me.
- I feel passionate about Singapore.

The more Singaporeans and PRs are able to say these, the higher the level of Engaged Citizenry in Singapore, and the greater the commitment and effectiveness of our communities to our city. I am convinced that Engaged Citizenry is one of the most important key performance indicators which a country's leaders can strive for and attain, be it in Singapore or otherwise.

What have we covered so far? One, moving forward, we need to forge new paths rather than to follow footsteps. Two, to do so, we need new flying instruments. Like the X-ray and the MRI, we need both tactical, process-based measures and we need strategic, behavioural-based ones. We need a mix of leading and lagging indicators. Three, we need new concepts. Population segments to think about our citizens and PRs, Engaged Citizens as a target to strive and shoot for, and Citizen Relationship Management or CRM as a new discipline that will enable Singapore to strategically and systematically build and attain Engaged Citizenry. What else do we need, for Singapore to be a Global City of Distinction and to be the Best Home for All?

GLOBAL CITY OF DISTINCTION AND BEST HOME FOR ALL: DIFFERENT STROKES FOR DIFFERENT FOLKS

Basically, we need different strokes for different folks. Just like every customer segment needs to be differently targeted, marketed and catered to, so do different population segments. In June last year, *The Business Times* published an article I wrote, titled "Take a good look at the 'Soul of the City'".

The article talked about how city planners and policy makers in cities and communities need to take a serious look at behavioural economic concepts and approaches and put them into practice, such that the cities and communities which they lead will become better places to live, work and play.

In a nutshell, the Soul of a City is determined by the collective experiences and responses of its citizens to three sub-indices relating to Engaged Citizenry, Emotional Well-Being and Personal Expression. The higher the Soul score, the more endearing a city to its residents, the greater the likelihood that residents will flourish in the city, achieve their dreams and contribute strongly to the city's achievements and outputs. Soul, an "outcome" measure, can be proactively impacted by what one calls "driver" measures. An "outcome" measure, by the way, is a measure or score (usually quantitative) that reflects the overall assessment of a product, service or situation on an overall basis, after taking everything into consideration. "Outcome" measures could reflect a state of being (e.g., overall satisfaction with life in Singapore) or be an indicator of likely behaviour in the future (such as the willingness to recommend Singapore as a great place to settle in). "Driver" measures on the other hand are factors that impact the "outcome measure". Most times multiple drivers impact the "outcome" measure, each usually having a differing extent of impact; "Driver measures may differ from time to time, depending on the circumstances surrounding the moment and depending on the population segments one is performing the analysis on".

A talk on Soul will take a full hour by itself. As we do not have the luxury of time today, let me quickly provide you a simple analysis of what the primary drivers of Soul are for some population segments in Singapore, as measured by our survey of 1,500 nationally-representative, randomly-sampled Singaporeans in August 2008. Jobs. Jobs. Jobs. At this very moment, employment is the most important driver for Soul for most population segments in Singapore (See Table 2). For other population segments, like the 40–59 age group, it is Community Basics in the form of Social Infrastructure, like the availability of quality healthcare and affordable housing. For the 60s and above age group, it is Prosperity which

Table 2 Employment is the top concern for most Singaporeans across the board

Different Strokes for Different Folks

By Education Levels	Primary Driver for Soul
University	Jobs
Polytechnic	Jobs
O & A Levels, ITE	Jobs
PSLE & below	Jobs

By Employment Status	Primary Driver for Soul
Employed	Jobs
Not Employed / Dependent	Jobs

By Age	Primary Driver for Soul
15–24	Jobs
25–39	Jobs
40–59	Community Basics
60 & above	Prosperity

By House Type	Primary Driver for Soul
1–3 room HDB	Jobs
4 room HDB	Jobs
5–exec HDB	Jobs
Private	Community Basics

relates to basic needs like Food & Shelter and Health & Wealth. For Singaporeans living in private housing, it is Community Basics in the form of Basic Infrastructure like Roads, Highways, the Public Transportation System, the Educational System and aspects of the Environment like the quality of air, water and the beauty of our physical settings.

CONCLUSION

In conclusion, what is the big picture? I think we need to forge new paths. We need new flying instruments, and we need new concepts like Population Segments, Engaged Citizenry, Citizen Relationship Management; and we need different strokes for different folks. In the last decade or so, social scientists and talent cartographers like Richard Florida have told us that the world is "spiky", that the most talented and mobile will trend toward cities and communities where they can best put their talents to their best use every single day, where they can continuously achieve their goals in their work and lives, and where they can provide and ensure the very best of environment for their families and loved ones. Gallup's research, past and current, supports this hypothesis. Countries, cities and communities with high psychological capital and social capital in addition to good national, financial, and community infrastructure will be better able to attract, engage and retain the very best talents, especially those who are highly mobile. And these talents will lead the way in creating the next wave of innovation, creativity, business and economic success, and the sustainability of that success.

Already, Singapore plays at the apex of the world's stage in all aspects of national, financial and community infrastructure. Moving forward, for Singapore to further move up the food chain and be a super strong magnet for talents and businesses foreign and local, we must create a very high sense of Soul, Engaged Citizenry, Personal Expression and Well-Being on our shores, for all Singaporeans. We must create and build a very high sense of psychological and social capital. What do I mean? We need all segments of our Singapore population to flourish as best as they can, and for as many Singaporeans as we can to exhibit high psychological capital like hope, optimism, resiliency and self-efficacy. We also need high social capital in Singapore. Neighbour looking after neighbour. A caring, cohesive, civic minded spirit exhibited across our entire society. A strong spirit of giving back to society such that society and the city get better and stronger time after time. Cities and communities with high social capital have strong alignment, high community harmony, a healthy sense of civic-mindedness, integration, cohesion, and most importantly, the pride and passion in its citizens very much like the engaged citizen model we have just talked about.

Psychological and Social Capital are important concepts for Singapore to leverage and ace in our next lap. We need every Singaporean to be highly engaged, and to exhibit a strong sense of pride and passion for our country. When we are able to do so, combined with the outstanding success we have already attained in our national, financial and community infrastructure, we will be able to predict, with a high degree of confidence, Singapore's success into the next millennium. That, I believe, is the Heart of the Matter.

Can Singaporeans Afford a High-Cost Singapore?

CHAPTER 2

Can Singaporeans Afford a High-Cost Singapore?

KEVIN SCULLY

The conference held by the Institute of Policy Studies is timely and necessary. The world economy, global currency system and global capital markets are in disarray and we are in the midst of a major paradigm shift in terms of the global currency system, the global capital markets and the way businesses respond to globalisation.

Let me start by making three points and asking four questions to our panellists and participants:

The first point is that the rise in costs in Singapore was intentional and engineered to promote the economic restructuring and the upgrading of manufacturing and services that helped Singapore sustain strong Gross Domestic Product (GDP) and per capita income growth since independence. Singapore has successfully used this to move manufacturing and services sectors up the value chain.

The second point I would like to make is the high costs or rising costs, which resulted from the above-average GDP growth that Singapore has achieved in the past, is to be expected. Income growth should increase accordingly with rising costs and should be uniform among the various strata of society. The question of affordability also applies to investors in terms of whether Singapore remains cost-competitive for them.

My third point is how we should compare the high cost of living in Singapore. Should we be comparing Singapore to other cities or to countries instead? The Mercer Worldwide Cost of Living Index for expatriates provides us with a good guide as it ranks both countries and cities. For 2008, the three most expensive countries were Russia, UK and South Korea. Singapore ranked 11th. In Asia, the three most expensive countries were South Korea, Japan and China. The top three cities were Moscow, Tokyo and London, with Singapore ranked 13th. Among Asian cities, the top three were Tokyo, Seoul and Hong Kong. Singapore ranked fifth after Osaka, with Beijing and Shanghai placed sixth and seventh respectively. Using New York, ranked 22nd in the survey, as a benchmark, Singapore does not appear to be a high-cost centre to expatriates as a city or even as a country.

My four questions to help bring discussions forward are:

a) Has Singapore remained competitive in terms of attracting investments? The 2009 Doing Business Survey conducted by the World Bank ranked Singapore first. How did Singapore manage to achieve this ranking? It appears that cost was neither the only nor the most consideration. Was it our political stability and consistency of government policies? In the current crisis, we are also seeing an increase in the area of corporate frauds and loan defaults. Are the legal framework and a strong enforcement regime more important today than it was before? Should we be focusing on areas other than cost?

b) Is this strategy of using high costs to move up the value chain still relevant? The current global economic and financial crisis has exposed some weaknesses in Singapore's strategy of relying strongly on Foreign Direct Investments (FDIs). The multinational corporations (MNCs) appear to be good for the economy in an economic up cycle. In a down cycle, overseas investments are the first to be downsized and the capital returned to its home country. With the global economy in a long recession of maybe, one or two years, will growing protectionism affect Singapore's positioning as a regional hub? Would this make Singapore less attractive as a conduit into the region?

c) Should the government be investing in local small and medium enterprises (SMEs) to promote domestic industries rather than co-investing MNCs? Will that provide more long-term stability for the Singapore economy?

d) Our number one ranking in the Doing Business 2009 survey shows that MNCs still find high-cost Singapore competitive. Have wages and incomes kept pace with the growth in costs? Do Singaporeans have a choice on essential items like housing, healthcare, education and transportation?

CHAPTER 3

Magnetic Resonance Imaging: Alternative Approach Needed for Economy

INDERJIT SINGH

INTRODUCTION

The topic about a high-cost Singapore is indeed timely as we grapple with the issues caused by the worst downturn the world has ever seen. Singapore's issue is not only one caused by a recession, but also one complicated by a preceding era of rapid cost increases and very high inflation. Unless we can rapidly bring down our costs in Singapore for individuals and for companies, we will have a difficult time coming out of the downturn and we will see unprecedented corporate failures and personal hardships faced by Singaporeans. I say this because I do not see demand coming back fast or incomes of Singaporeans rising again for quite some time to come. The government has a challenge in handling both sides of an equation: income and demand on one side and cost on the other.

As Singapore continues to expand economically, the lack of space will drive business costs up. Another factor that is likely to add pressure on rising costs in Singapore is the government's plans to increase the country's population over the coming years. This will increase the demand for key factors of production, and the competition for factors of production will accelerate increasing business costs further. One argument to this is that high costs are inevitable in resource-scarce Singapore. We need to move up the value chain of businesses and not depend on lower value-added activities to drive our economy and earn our incomes. Everyone needs to upgrade their skills and businesses need to upgrade their capabilities and to engage in activities further up the value chain. This has been the direction the government has taken to transform our economy and our workforce. This is done by either focusing on skills upgrading or by bringing in foreign talent.

GROWTH-AT-ALL-COSTS POLICY

Could rising costs in Singapore be avoided? Is the government's growth-at-all-costs policy the most effective for Singapore? One implication of rising costs is the low viability of low-cost industries operating in Singapore. This is accentuated by more cost-competitive countries, such as China and Vietnam in the region. Consequently, the government has opted to move the level of economic activity in Singapore up the value chain and force lower value-added activities to relocate in lower-cost countries. At many levels, this is very much like the business outsourcing strategy that multinationals have adopted in decentralising production processes.

This was how most developed nations progressed when they experienced high costs. They looked elsewhere for their low-cost production needs to support their higher value-added activities in their respective home economies. With regard to textile, steel, automobiles and light electronics industries, there was a distinctive point in each industry's life cycle where it was more profitable to let another country provide the labour or to take over the production process. In East Asia, Taiwan and Korea have in the past been beneficiaries of declining Japanese industries. Leading economies move into higher value-added activities as their own cost structures rise, thus allowing their lower-cost partners to take over the lower value-added activities.

It is not surprising that Singapore, like other more-developed countries in the region, has adopted a similar strategy. However, the point of contention here is the rate at which this movement up the value chain has occurred in Singapore. From the United Nations Conference on Trade and Development (UNCTAD)'s Trade Development Report, the Manufacturing Value-Added (MVA) indicator gives the composition of a country's higher value-added activities in its aggregate production. Even though Singapore's MVA has risen rapidly, its productivity has grown at a lower rate thus showing that it has moved too quickly up the value chain without achieving equivalent improvements in efficiency (see Table 1).

Table 1 Singapore's rise in MVA does not commensurate with its productivity growth rates

Manufacturing Value-Added (MVA) in Selected Countries				
Country	MVA (% of world total)		MVA Ratio 2003/1980	Productivity Growth Rates (1980–2002) (%)
	1980	2003		
China	3.3	8.5	2.6	5.2
Taiwan	0.6	1.1	1.8	4.3
Korea	0.7	2.3	3.3	4.9
ASEAN 4	1.2	2.8	2.3	2
Developed Countries	64.5	73.3	1.1	1.6
Singapore	0.1	0.45	4.5	3.7

Source: UNCTAD

Using these statistics, Singapore's MVA, which was 0.1 percent of the world's share in 1980, had grown to 0.45 percent of the world's share by 2003. This means that Singapore's share of medium and high value-added activities in the world has increased to 4.5 times its 1980 share in these 23 years. Singapore's rate of transition is more than other developing Asian countries over the same time period with Korea increasing to 3.3 times, Taiwan to 1.8 times and the ASEAN Four (ASEAN Five excluding Singapore) to 2.3 times 1980 levels. Even China, which experienced an unprecedented level of industrialisation and technological adoption over this time period, increased its MVA to 2.6 times of 1980 levels. The group of developed countries' share of global MVA rose from 64.5 percent in 1980 to 73.3 percent in 2003, with latter numbers only 1.1 times of 1980 figures.

From the statistics, Singapore's transition from low value-added industries to high value-added sectors has exceeded the rate of other developed countries and has happened too rapidly. You may ask: why is this a problem? After all, having a higher MVA faster means we are progressing better and moreover; why should we turn away opportunities to upgrade ourselves? The point is that moving up the value chain has forced business costs in Singapore to rise (see Chart 1). Singapore has the highest unit business costs which had exceeded productivity rates and the rate of increase in Singapore's business costs from 2006 to 2008 is sharpest.

Chart 1 Business costs in Singapore rose at an extremely high rate between 2006 and 2008

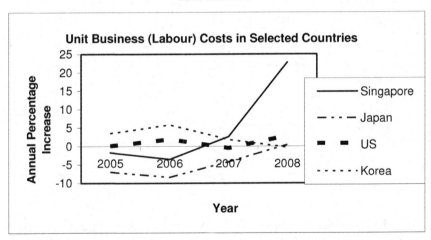

Source: International Labour Organization

From 2007 to 2008, unit labour costs in Singapore increased by 22.8 percent compared to 0.4 percent and 2.8 percent in Japan and US respectively. At the other end, Korea's unit labour costs fell by 0.3 percent during the same period. To emphasise the severity of the problem, the rising labour costs in Singapore were not directly a result of higher productivity. From the productivity growth rates released by the International Labour

Organization, Singapore's productivity increased by 3.7 percent from 1980 to 2002, suggesting that its productive efficiency was increasing at a slower rate than its MVA growth as well as its rising business costs. It is therefore moving too quickly up the value chain of activities. Singapore has the sharpest rise in rankings from the 46th position in 2004 to the 13th position in 2008 (see Table 2).

Table 2 Singapore rose from 46th position to 13th position in a ranking of the world's most expensive cities between 2004 and 2008

Ranking of Expensive Cities		
2008	Country	2004
1	Moscow	3
2	Tokyo	1
3	London	2
4	Oslo	15
5	Seoul	7
6	Hong Kong	5
7	Copenhagen	8
8	Geneva	6
9	Zurich	9
10	Milan	13
11	Osaka	4
12	Paris	17
13	Singapore	46
14	Tel Aviv	33
15	Sydney	20

Source: Mercer's 2008 Cost of Living Survey

DISLOCATION OF INDUSTRIES AND CAPABILITIES

Why does the rate of transition matter? After all, is it not a positive reflection of Singapore's technological capabilities if our rate of moving up the value chain is faster than other Asian economies? The implication of a high rate of development is that it dislodges Singapore's economy, workforce and other infrastructure. A slower rate of development would encourage domestic industries to improve on their capabilities and technologies. This would keep industries in Singapore for a longer period of time. The textile industry in Belgium is a good example. Till today, it has a turnover of 6.6 billion Euros and has been able to maintain its volume of output despite lower-cost competition from other countries and the strengthening of the Euro. The relative good performance and continued viability of the textile industry in Belgium is a result of a high degree of specialisation and more importantly, due to the increasing efficiency of high capital-intensive enterprises. By being capital-intensive, production processes are automated and highly advanced. This has resulted in increasing returns to scale for the Belgian textile industry. The same output is achieved by only a third of the workforce compared to 30 years ago.

Singapore, on the other hand, had moved on to newer industries quickly such as electronics production instead of developing the competencies of its domestic textile industries. Textile companies were forced to relocate in lower-cost countries and Singapore lost out on potential dividends from a viable industry. The approach had led Singapore to lose many of its core competencies each time it started afresh with a new industry. The result was the dislocation of relevant infrastructure, skills workers had gained and the knowledge required of each industry. If Singapore had focused on productivity and innovation, it could have stretched capabilities and allowed lower value-added industries, like textiles, to be viable by being highly automated. This would have allowed Singapore to keep, and benefit from, its core competencies for a longer period. The government's approach was to de-incentivise companies from trying to keep many of what the government considered as 'no-longer-attractive' capabilities in Singapore so that land and manpower can be freed up for a newer group of industries.

IMPACT OF POPULATION GROWTH

As I mentioned earlier, while cost increases are inevitable, the government could have slowed down the rate of increase. Here, the issue of population growth is another point of contention. Based on the United Nations' World Urbanization Prospects Report, Singapore's rate of population growth exceeded that of most other small countries. From 1995 to 2005, Singapore grew at an average of 2.285 percent, while Luxembourg and Belgium grew at 1.73 and 0.265 percent respectively. Even densely-populated entities like Hong Kong and Monaco grew at 1.495 and 0.98 percent respectively. Singapore's average population growth clearly increased at an over-rapid pace between 1995 and 2005, a phenomenon that had added pressure to the rising costs in Singapore. However, a healthy rate of population growth is needed to develop a reliable workforce since population growth is essential. Given Singapore's Total Fertility Rate and immigration rate, the government should aim to achieve an average annual population increase of about 1.5 percent over the next 10 years to attain a total population of about 5.2 million. An accelerated rate of population growth may have drastic implications for the cost structure in Singapore.

THE DOUBLE WHAMMY OF THE POPULATION POLICY

While I can understand the rationale of the population policy and that of bringing in foreign labour and talent to work in our companies, I feel we may have been too impatient in wanting to see results. As I mentioned in Parliament during my Budget speech last year, we have been ramping up the population relentlessly in the last couple of years. It is like we want a tree, but are not willing to wait for it to grow. Singapore's "instant tree" mentality is pushing the pace of population growth at unrealistic rates. As we bring in more and more people, many from India and China, not just at the top level of talent, but also at various levels including unskilled workers, we depress the wages of Singaporeans. However, our costs continue to go up, because of imported inflation, and because of our policies. Hence, we cause a double whammy for Singaporeans who have no choice but to live with the high cost of living while having to accept lower wages. This is especially so for lower-income Singaporeans (see Chart 2).

Chart 2 Real wage increases of various income groups in Singapore

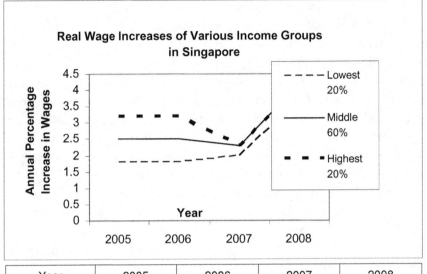

Year	2005	2006	2007	2008
Inflation Rate	0.5	1.0	2.1	5.5

Source: Singapore Department of Statistics

We had also created a problem for companies in the long term by allowing companies to access low-cost labour with a very liberal population policy and a liberal foreign worker policy. In the short term, companies benefited because they got access to workers easily and in the long term, there was no impetus for companies to inject greater productivity, innovation and automation to create real added value to the economy. We continue to rely on input factors, especially labour, to keep the economy going. Paul Krugman explained this fallacy as he sought to dispel the apparent myth of the Asian miracle. He asserted that East Asian growth models, including Singapore's, were based on mobilising resources rather than on increasing efficiency. As a result, the Singapore growth model has been predominantly built upon increased inputs, primarily of labour and capital, and not innovation and productivity. According to Krugman, unless production processes are made more efficient, diminishing marginal returns will make the use of more inputs unproductive. I believe this will be a big problem for us as cost continues to increase in Singapore because of our limited resources.

THE ALTERNATIVE APPROACH

An underlying problem is the government's growth-at-all cost policy. As a result, the rapid changes in the structure of the economy made it difficult for Singaporeans and firms to cope. How could we have otherwise managed our economic development without applying artificial restrictions which may not work? How could we have avoided the overheating of our economy and inflation drivers which are under our control?

Firstly, we could have avoided a policy that fuelled an already overheated situation. The approach taken in the last few years before the financial meltdown was to allow rapid growth where possible. We attracted many new companies by giving very attractive incentives, which in most cases favoured foreign companies and disadvantaged local ones. Secondly, we fuelled the economy in good times by trying to build two integrated resorts (IRs) at the same time, by trying to build a sports hub and by building roads and other infrastructure. We tried to do everything at the same time and as a result of market forces, costs went up and rapidly too.

A moderation of growth rates would have eased the pressure on resources and on costs in Singapore and hence, prevented a heating of the economy. For instance, the government may have chosen to pursue the development of one integrated resort at a time instead of two. It could also have opted to do some of its infrastructural development and government expenditure in lean years instead of concentrating these resources in boom years. All of these factors added to a bubble, which was already growing due to a healthy economy. The government could attempt to cool and prevent overheating of the economy in boom years instead. In the last economic cycle, the government pursued a reverse trend and made cost increases unrealistic. For example, all efforts to cool the 1996 property bubble were undone within two years, 2006 and 2007. Singapore has not recovered from this and its economy will be dealt with a bigger blow in this economic downturn.

With regard to labour, I supported the policy of greater liberalisation of our population policy and foreign worker policies. However, we should

31

have moderated our policies. Companies will no doubt have problems getting workers. We should have compelled them to have a good mix of foreign and local workers and incentivise companies to move up the value chain and focus on productivity to attain real improvement in the quality of our economic growth factors. We could have incentivised companies to be more innovative and improve productivity instead of giving them the easy way out with easy access to foreign workers as an alternative to local workers. How could we have done this? Perhaps by giving enough tax incentives and grants to companies as a leveller so that it will make hiring foreign workers not much cheaper than hiring locals.

We may have to start thinking of a minimum wage system that applies to both local and foreign workers. While painful in the beginning, all of us will learn about the importance of productivity and innovation to do more with less. Such a system will make our companies stronger, made better use of Singaporean workers and contribute better to the economy as Singaporeans remain employed and are being paid sufficiently to cope with the higher cost of living. This might also address the complaints of employers on local workers, which is, that they are not willing to do jobs that are made available. From what I understand, they are not willing because the wages would not be sufficient to make ends meet and they continue to leave low-paying jobs to look for better-paying ones. This may not be the best approach but how does one get by when one's income is lower than one's expenditure?

SUSTAINABLE MODEL OF GROWTH FOR THE FUTURE

What is a sustainable model that Singapore can adopt? The government's strategy should be to promote innovation and strengthen local enterprises by building their capabilities. The MNC (multinational corporation) approach that has been the focus of Singapore's development should no longer be the driver of the economy as it will probably not be feasible for much longer. Developing countries with lower operating costs such as China and India will soon catch up by enhancing their core competencies, making Singapore less viable for many economic activities except for the service industries. Had we focused on the capacity-building of local enterprises, the government would have ensured that they keep moving up the value chain while they internationalise. Local companies will try to make things work and remain in Singapore for the long haul. I fear the time when multinational corporations (MNCs) will move out at a faster rate than we can bring newer ones in. Another concern is that levels of job creation for Singaporeans will be low while increasing numbers of foreign talent will be brought in to jump-start new industries and companies. As the net flow of MNCs is in an outwards direction, our local companies may not grow fast enough to keep the economy afloat or to create jobs to employ those retrenched by the exiting MNCs. We must step up our efforts to help local enterprises to become more competitive in a high-cost environment.

It is not too late to make changes. New opportunities will arise where older ones are lost in this downturn. However, these new opportunities must be effectively utilised using the correct model of growth. The suggested model should involve a moderation of cost while Singapore's core competencies are strengthened. This will allow Singapore to keep its industries for a longer period of time and to benefit from their potential specialisation and technology. Such a model would allow Singapore to grow at lower costs. By developing its human capital and the capabilities of its domestic industries, there may be fewer limits to the country's growth. We must avoid "boom-and-bust" policies. Instead, the government should tap on its ample resources to keep the economy afloat in a downturn while resisting pumping more into the economy when the economy is doing well. While we cannot control external factors, we can definitely control some of the factors that lead to inflation.

CONCLUSION

While we are all proud that Singapore progressed from a Third World to a First World nation within one generation, the question is: at what cost? While costs went up rapidly, nearing those of most developed countries, our wages did not catch up as fast for a significant group of Singaporeans. Their wages remained close to those of developing nations. This mismatch is something the government needs to address. We need to find the right balance of the cost of living we can afford and the type of capabilities our population can develop.

CHAPTER 4

Reaching Out to Low-Income Groups in Singapore

LAURENCE LIEN

INTRODUCTION

I am here to give my personal views, which are influenced by my being at the National Volunteer and Philanthropy Centre (NVPC), on the social perspectives of the issue, "Can Singaporeans afford a high-cost Singapore?" In short, the answer is "yes for some, and no for others". The issue is definitely a lot more complicated. I will first look at some factual information on how Singaporeans are coping with a high cost of living, and go on to what we can do about this.

FACTS AND REALITY

First, high-income households are getting richer and low-income households are getting poorer (see Table 1). The average income for employed households excluding retiree households decreased by 1.3 percent from 2000 to 2005. The reason for this is globalisation and having an open economy. This means we are price-takers and increasingly there are two separate labour markets, one for well-paid high-skilled individuals and another for low-skilled individuals, who have to compete with the huge supply of lower-wage workers from developing countries.

Table 1 High-income households are getting richer and low-income households are getting poorer

Average Monthly Per Capita Household Income from Work by Deciles

Percentile	All Households				Employed Households			
	2000	2004	2005	Avg. Annual Change (%), 2000–2005	2000	2004	2005	Avg. Annual Change (%), 2000–2005
Total	1,430	1,570	1,640	2.7	1,570	1,750	1,820	3.0
1st–10th	20	0	0	-	290	280	270	-1.3
11th–20th	340	290	280	-3.7	490	490	510	0.6
21th–30th	540	530	540	-	660	690	700	1.3
31st–40th	720	740	750	0.9	820	880	900	1.8
41st–50th	910	950	980	1.5	1,010	1,080	1,120	2.1
51st–60th	1,130	1,200	1,250	1.9	1,230	1,330	1,390	2.4
61st–70th	1,410	1,510	1,580	2.4	1,500	1,640	1,720	2.7
71st–80th	1,780	1,940	2,030	2.7	1,880	2,080	2,180	3.0
81st–90th	2,420	2,700	2,830	3.2	2,530	2,870	3,000	3.4
91st–100th	5,080	5,840	6,150	3.9	5,280	6,110	6,440	4.1

Source: General Household Survey 2005: Transport, Overseas Travel, Household and Housing Characteristics

The Gini coefficient (see Table 2), which is the standard measure of income inequality, has worsened over time and is likely to stay as a consequence of the increasing cost of living.

Table 2 Singapore's Gini coefficient has also become higher

Measures of Inequality in Per Capita Household Income from Work

	All Households[2]		Employed Households[3]	
	Gini Coefficient[1]	Ratio of Average Per Capita Income of Top 20% to Lowest 20%	Gini Coefficient[1]	Ratio of Average Per Capita Income of Top 20% to Lowest 20%
2000	0.490	20.9	0.442	10.0
2001	0.493	19.5	0.455	11.0
2002	0.505	25.4	0.455	11.2
2003	0.512	28.1	0.458	11.4
2004	0.517	29.6	0.463	11.6
2005	0.522	31.9	0.468	12.1

1 The Gini coefficient takes values from zero to one. The more unequal the income distribution, the larger the Gini coefficient.

2 Based on ranking of all resident households by per capita monthly household income from work.

3 Based on ranking of resident households with income earners by per capita monthly household income from work.

Source: General Household Survey 2005: Transport, Overseas Travel, Household and Housing Characteristics

Furthermore, low-income households face a double whammy as inflation has also generally been higher for them. In recent years, inflation was generally higher for the lower-income households (see Table 3). The lowest 20 percent has suffered higher rates of inflation than the other income groups. Although 2007 was better, in 2008 we saw higher food prices, higher housing rental rates and higher transport prices that might have hit the lower-income households quite badly.

Table 3 Inflation hits certain groups more badly than others

Inflation For Households by Income Groups
(Percentage change over previous year)

	2004	2005	2006	2007
Lowest 20%	2.3	1.3	1.8	2.0
Middle 60%	1.5	0.6	1.1	2.0
Highest 20%	0.3	-0.1	0.4	2.3

Source: General Expenditure Survey, 2003

What is the impact of high prices? For the high-income Singaporeans, real wages have been rising more rapidly so they can cope better with the high cost of living. For the lower-income individuals, many would struggle to meet ends meet. The adverse social impact on the lower strata in society, for example decreased self-esteem, stress on the individual and his family, and the threat of a permanent underclass emerging, cannot be underestimated. These families need help to get out of their poverty trap.

Excluding the high-income households, expenditure has been increasing faster than income from 1998 to 2003 (see Table 4). This is not sustainable.

Table 4 Expenditure has been rising faster than income

Income and Expenditure Changes for Working Households
(Per capita percentage change per annum)

	1993–1998	1998–2003	
	Income	Income	Expenditure
Lowest 20%	5.5	0.8	1.6
2nd Quintile	7.5	2.0	2.6
3rd Quintile	8.4	2.1	2.5
4th Quintile	8.5	2.6	3.3
Highest 20%	7.8	3.7	1.8

Source: General Expenditure Survey, 2003

To an extent, an ageing population may explain this. An increasingly greater number of the households in the bottom 20 percent would include retiree households. However, the rate of expenditure has also been increasing faster than that of income for the middle 60 percent of the population.

IMPACT OF HIGH COST AND INFLATION

A consequence of expenditure rising faster than income is that people will be saving less and possibly insufficiently for the future (see Table 5). Already, the low-income household has a diminished ability to save. A retirement studies conducted by AXA, a financial institution, showed that Singaporeans rely heavily on their Central Provident Fund (CPF) savings for retirement income and for many, their CPF savings would not give them a sufficiently high income-replacement ratio if they do not have other sources of savings.

Even government rebates as an income supplement may not be sufficient (see Table 5). Expenditure was still greater than income for the bottom 40 percent. One concern is the current low expenditure on merit goods, which are items that are deemed necessary by a society's norms and standards. Looking at the types of consumer durables owned by the lowest-income households for example, figures show that half the households in the lowest bracket have air-conditioners at home. This gives the

Table 5 Government rebates as an income supplement may not suffice

Income and Expenditure for Households by Income Groups
($ Per Capita)

2003	Income	Income + Rebates	Expenditure	Savings
Lowest 20%	315	339	568	-229
2nd Quintile	669	693	712	-19
3rd Quintile	1043	1068	864	204
4th Quintile	1615	1640	1129	511
Highest 20%	3857	3883	1537	2346

Source: General Expenditure Survey, 2003

impression that the low-income group may not be that badly off. However, one cannot assume that people are rational and wise in their spending choices as we often spend too much on things we do not need, and not enough on things that we do need. In my opinion, expenditure on merit goods, be it on education or health, might be affected for low-income families.

For retirees, real wealth will get eroded if inflation is high, particularly during economic downturns when returns from risky asset classes are poor. Increased longevity suggests more is needed to meet longer-term needs. A higher cost of living could also have an impact on fertility decisions.

What could we do about this? I am making assumptions that we are price-takers for our labour markets, and that there is nothing significant we can do about income levels and that we need to keep jobs. There are three things we could do: having government income-redistribution programmes, lowering costs and encouraging private giving in the form of volunteerism and philanthropy.

INCOME REDISTRIBUTION

Government subsidies do help the lower-income group. Singaporeans are no longer experiencing high rates of income growth like we did from 1993 to 1998, when almost everybody was a winner. In a competitive world with free trade, Singapore specialised in products with comparative advantage. Although we can create a larger economic pie for the nation, there are inevitably gainers and losers. There is a need to redistribute the gains from the winners to the losers through mechanisms such as the Workfare Income Supplement (WIS) (see Chart 1).

However, one problem with understanding the impact of redistribution is, the monies are given for different purposes and are not entirely fungible. This is true even if you give cash, with the use not restricted for a particular type of expenditure. We know from behavioural economics that people practise mental accounting. They would treat permanent income differently from temporary income, with each individual having a different marginal propensity to consume. In addition, consumption baskets may also differ from individual to individual. Hence, monies from a Goods and Services Tax (GST) offset package may go to the purchase of a lottery ticket, for example.

Chart 1   The Workfare Income Supplement will aid Singaporeans who need the most help

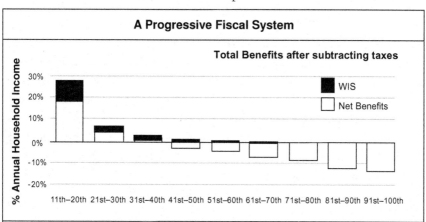

Benefits other than WIS for households include:
- GST Offset Package: GST Credits, Senior Citizens' Bonus, top-ups to Post Secondary Education Account (PSEA), Utilities-Save rebates, Service and Conservancy Charges rebates, rental rebates and property tax rebates; and
- Surplus Sharing measures announced in Budget 2008: Growth Dividends, additional PSEA top-ups, personal income tax rebates and top-ups to Medisave accounts.

Taxes paid by households include:
- Personal income tax, goods and service tax, motor-vehicle related taxes, foreign maid levy and property tax.
- 1st–10th percentiles have no household income.

Source: Ministry Of Finance Estimates

Government income redistribution works only to a limited extent. Government subsidy and redistribution schemes cannot be too customised to cater to the unique situation of each individual because that will create administrative inefficiencies. Neither can the government be too generous in its payouts to cater for the worst case because that will make aid far too costly. The latter will also create an entitlement mentality and rent-seeking behaviour. Payouts also have the effect of damaging self-esteem and self-confidence.

I see aid from the government like a big stone one uses to fill a container, but one still need small stones to fill in the gaps. That is where non-profit organisations come in.

LOWERING COSTS

With regards to keeping costs low, I think we need to have two Singapores in terms of costs. What do I mean by this? Let me give examples. In Singapore we can spend $250 per square foot for a HDB flat or $2,500 per square foot for a condominium. We can spend $3 on chicken rice at the hawker centre or $30 at a restaurant. We can spend $4.60 for a medical consultation for a child at SingHealth polyclinic or $60 for a paediatrician. There are choices. If we want to pay more, there are very high-cost options but if you want to pay less, there are good low-cost options. The focus of public policy should be to focus on items that form the largest proportions of expenditure for the low-income households such as food, transport, and housing, and healthcare, which has been the fastest growing item. (See Table 6).

Table 6 Food and Housing expenditures take up a greater proportion of household income among the lowest quintile of Singapore households

Average Monthly Household Expenditure

	1998 All (%)	2003 All (%)	2003 Lowest 20% (%)
Food	23.7	21.3	28.3
Clothing & Footwear	4.1	3.6	2.6
Housing	21.9	22.4	28.1
Transport & Communication	22.7	21.4	14.2
Education & Stationery	6.8	7.8	5.7
Health Care	3.3	5.1	7.0
Recreation & Others	16.9	17.8	13.0
Non-Assignable	0.7	0.7	1.1

Source: General Expenditure Survey, 2003

ENCOURAGE PRIVATE GIVING

Lastly, we must encourage private giving. There is a huge capacity for growth in this area, even in bad times. When compared to the United States of America, levels of private giving in Singapore appear to be low and show scope to grow more (see Table 7). Although figures of private giving in Singapore do not include donations to organisations not classified as Institutes of Public Character (IPCs) — such as religious institutions — their inclusion would still be much lower than the 2.2 percent of Gross Domestic Product (GDP) for total giving in the US.

Table 7 Singapore can do more in terms of volunteerism

Giving and Volunteerism in Singapore and the US

Singapore	US
• Total giving to Institutions of Public Character (IPC) was 0.34% of GDP in 2007 • Formal + Informal volunteerism rate was 16.9% (2008)	• Total charitable giving was 2.2% of GDP in 2007 • Formal Volunteerism rate was 26.2% (2007)
Sources: Commissioner of Charities Annual Report 2007, "Individual Giving Survey" 2008, NVPC; and Giving USA Report 2008, "Volunteering in the US" (2008), Corporation for National & Community Service, US	

We should also encourage more volunteerism because giving should not just be about money. I do not think giving money is a trade-off to giving time. According to surveys done by the NVPC, volunteers give four times more than non-volunteers in donations. Giving is not just about saving money for the government. We should encourage private giving because there are limitations to what the state can do. Firstly, as I mentioned earlier, government policy cannot be too customised. Secondly, I think the people sector can do some things better than the government. People-sector organisations have the moral authority to address difficult social issues. A dollar given by a concerned neighbour is very different from a dollar given by your Community Development Council (CDC). People-sector organisa-tions can also be a rich source of innovation and experimentation that go beyond national policy and ideology. Thirdly, we need to cater to different and holistic needs. The government tends to focus on material and physical needs because it has a comparative advantage in doing large-scale wealth redistribution. However, a human being also needs social, emotional and spiritual support.

CONCLUSION

We need to show that as a society, we care. There are discussions about the need to build high social capital, engaged citizenry and active citizenry to build national pride and passion. A key test of a mature society is how one would treat the less fortunate. A happy society is one where people share and give. Individual happiness is the social fabric of the society and is something that we need to keep intact. For society to continue to progress, we cannot afford to have the divides between those who do well and those who struggle to just get by. We often talk a lot about the poor having an entitlement mentality. The wealthy can also have an entitlement mentality. They may believe that they deserve everything that they get, and everything that they earn. And I am especially concerned that younger Singaporeans who do well are a bit more ostentatious and less compassionate than older Singaporeans. The current financial crisis is a great opportunity for Singaporeans to show that they care. This is my last point and I am confident that many of us will step up to the plate just like we did in previous recessions. The year 2001 was a recession year but donations to IPCs went up by 17 percent from the previous year. The current recession is worse than the previous one, but I hope those who can afford to give will do so. If the government is drawing down on national reserves, we and our families should likewise consider giving more as well.

SECTION **III**

Can Singaporeans Remain Rooted?

CHAPTER 5

Can Singaporeans Remain Rooted?

NORMAN VASU

Let me begin with some data. Citizens make up 65 percent of Singapore's total population, and together with permanent residents (PRs), they add up to approximately 75 percent. The remaining 25 percent consists of foreigners who are living, working or studying here. The influx of foreign talent has been seen to be a necessary top-up to the labour pool because of the impending long-term decline of numbers with Singapore's low fertility rate, the increased demand for manpower (certainly before last year's economic crisis unfolded), and the belief that foreigners inject new ideas and dynamism to the country. Coupled with this influx of foreign talent is the issue of the loss of top talent among Singaporeans of about 1,000 people every year. Singapore is a highly globalised country, and Singaporeans are very aware of what the outside world offers when they travel, work and study abroad. This foreign influx coupled with exposure from the outside, naturally brings us to the critical nature of the question of rootedness among Singaporeans.

There are several questions often raised with regard to the rootedness debate in Singapore. For example, one of them is the question involving how we can develop rootedness. Dr Gillian Koh from the Institute of Policy Studies wrote about rootedness last year in an article. She said that to encourage rootedness, perhaps an active sense of belonging could be cultivated: if people have the sense that they have a greater say in how the country develops, they may feel they have a stake in it. There is also the need to develop physical familiarity and also a passive belonging where

Singaporeans feel that they benefit from the job and career opportunities as well as the modern conveniences and quality of life available here.

Other questions commonly asked in the rootedness debate include: Should we even be concerned with rootedness? Does the presence of foreigners actually affect the sense of rootedness among Singaporeans? For instance, do they feel like foreigners in their own country?

While I am not suggesting that these are not important questions or aspects of the rootedness debate, what tends to be forgotten is the idea of rootedness itself. What does it mean to be rooted, or more specifically, what does it mean for Singaporeans to be rooted to Singapore? Does the act of paying taxes, or doing national service, or not giving up one's citizenship mean that one is rooted?

Also, why does the benchmark for rootedness in Singapore appear often to be based on the worst-case scenario of one's willingness to fight and die for one's country? Should policies be formulated based on such extremes? Finally, discussions on rootedness tend to focus on the negative aspects of why Singaporeans leave. Perhaps we should look at why people stay or feel a sense of belonging in the first place. Looking at rootedness in a more positive light may help offer new threads to this discussion.

CHAPTER 6

Singaporean Rootedness: Taking Stock and Moving Forward

TAN ERN SER

INTRODUCTION: WHAT IS ROOTEDNESS?

Let us begin by exploring three different contexts in which we can apply the concept of rootedness. First, rootedness can be associated with living in a small town. Some years ago I managed to visit quite a number of small towns across America. There I witnessed a sense of community, of people who seemed to be quite happy and relaxed where they felt that they were living among friends and relatives. Second, rootedness is related to the sense of autobiography, or the place where one is raised. Personally, I was brought up in something akin to a slum area near the Subordinate Courts in the city, and while I have memories and some nostalgia relating to that place, it certainly is not where I would want to be rooted to. The third context relates to the famous example of the Jewish diaspora. The Jewish diaspora has spread out for the last 2,000 years to Europe and the United States and other parts of the world, but the Jews remain very much rooted to their homeland. The Jewish situation is also problematic in that the Palestinians claim the same piece of land in the Middle East. Both groups are just as rooted to this place but these are somewhat mutually exclusive sentiments.

What is rootedness? It is the quality or state of having roots, of being firmly established, settled or entrenched in a place. There is the sense that one is in tune with the socio-cultural world associated with a particular locality. It refers therefore to both the social world and the physical location. Rootedness provides the basis of a socio-psychological anchor, attachment and affiliation, and provides continuous nourishment towards that end. Like a tree, one receives nourishment from that source. Another point about rootedness is the connection to the past, present, and future of the people and place in which one is rooted. This provides the basis for the struggle for national survival and well-being. For our purpose here, I choose to think of this concept as rootedness to the nation with implications for national survival — the nation of Singapore, rather than a sense of affiliation to certain districts in Singapore like Queenstown or Toa Payoh.

Robert Bellah and his team explored some key characteristics of rootedness in their book titled *Habits of the Heart: Individualism and Commitment in American Life*[1]. Rootedness is about identity, a sense of belongingness and emotional attachment. A person's identity is formed in his or her growing years and by connecting with others. These definitions have been used quite a bit in Singapore. Another characteristic of rootedness relates to the place where one is willing to invest his or her ambition and future. Are we willing today, to invest our ambition and future in Singapore? That is a question of rootedness in Singapore. Further, when we say that one is rooted to a place, he or she would also be willing to link his or her self-interest to the public good of the community therein. Do we have a sense that we and our fellow citizens are actually in the same boat?

Rootedness also operates on the logic of community rather than the marketplace. Earlier in this conference, the speaker Mr Peter Ong had suggested that respondents to a survey on the "soul" of Singapore had suggested that their well-being would be most heavily influenced by their job. I disagree with that notion. There is a distinction between the utilitarian world of work and the expressive world of friendly community. Rootedness has to do with the expressive world of friendly community, where we should feel that we are among friends and people who care for us, and

---

[1] Bellah, Robert *et. al.* (1985). *Habits of the Heart: Individualism and Commitment in American Life*. Berkeley and Los Angeles, California: University of California Press.

amongst people whom we are willing to contribute to and invest in. Rootedness is also associated with a generosity of spirit where citizens are willing to engage in nurturing connectedness with others in the community. There is a sense of owing a debt, or debts, to society.

Rootedness has to do with community, connectedness, commitment, involvement and memory. This relates to a sense of engagement in the nation and a desire to bring about a better future for this nation. Rootedness is also about having a common purpose and a national life which transcends particular interests. Rootedness is not just about whether we get jobs, but whether there is a sense of common or national purpose. Rootedness can also manifest in exclusion or an "island" mentality, as can sometimes be seen in small towns. This may not seem like the best attitude in the age of globalisation, for even as we are rooted, even as we love this place and country, are we willing to allow others to share in what we have?

Rootedness is also about being tied to a place, even for the mobile, the cosmopolitan. I believe it is possible, even if you are cosmopolitan, working elsewhere, to feel rooted to Singapore. While we may not have the same history and culture as the Jews, there is nothing to say that we cannot be rooted to Singapore while we are overseas in places like Perth and Toronto.

WHAT BRINGS ABOUT ROOTEDNESS?

What brings about rootedness? Rootedness takes place when one moves from a self-interested position and mentality to that which prompts an interest in the common good of the larger community. I believe that people will be rooted if they feel a sense of security, comfort and can have a decent quality of life and well-being for themselves and their children. Most would not want to be in a place that does not even have the basic necessities. People also want to be in a place, a community which has an affirming and encouraging culture. In Singapore, we tend not to rejoice with those who succeed and are sometimes quite dismissive of small successes. Perhaps if we affirm one another more, we would feel more "together" and hopefully this would result in an increased sense of rootedness. Correspondingly, community support, a sense of membership in that one is not marginalised because of one's ethnicity or class and involvement also encourages rootedness and especially so in multi-ethnic, multicultural Singapore.

Rootedness could, on the other hand, result from shared negative experiences which lead to the need for self-preservation. The Jewish diaspora has the collective experience of discrimination and exclusion. The Jews and Palestinians can both relate to a collective sense of suffering injustice. In addition, contestation for a certain geographical terrain can increase the sense of rootedness within the related community of peoples where there was not much of a connection before.

WHAT ARE OUR EXPECTATIONS OF ROOTEDNESS?

I will address this question of "our expectations" from the perspective of the government, and what the government expects of Singaporeans in terms of rootedness. The Singapore 21 (S21) initiative, inaugurated in 1997, had five key ideas. First, the S21 vision proclaimed the principle that "Every Singaporean Matters". I believe that if we did abide by this, Singaporeans would be rooted, or at least we would be in the process of getting there. The second and third principles were that we need strong families and opportunities for all. The fourth is the Singapore Heartbeat, of feeling passionately about Singapore, because this is where we find our roots and our future; to think of Singapore as our home, a place worth living, fighting and dying for. Rootedness is much more than just money, benefits, or jobs and has to do with our whole sense of well-being and identity. The fifth principle set out the desire to inculcate active citizenship, or allowing citizens to make a difference to society. S21 had to do with thinking about Singapore as home.

In 2007, the Committee on National Education came up with the 3H framework aimed at strengthening "heartware" and rootedness. The three Hs are "Head, Heart and Hands". "Head" referred to developing an understanding of the challenges facing Singapore and what it meant to be a Singaporean. "Heart" referred to an emotional connection to the Singapore story and a love for the nation. "Hands" referred to giving back to society, and having a part to contribute to and create Singapore's future. The 3H framework was not very different from S21, but was couched in a way that was more accessible to students and teachers.

HOW ROOTED ARE WE?

How are we doing in terms of rootedness? A 2005 IPS Survey on Rootedness conducted by Brenda Yeoh, Gillian Koh and me defined rootedness in terms of five components. The first is a spatial or physical familiarity, or a certain fondness for a place. For instance, I understand that people who were raised in Tiong Bahru like Tiong Bahru for its nice, friendly and relaxed atmosphere. The second relates to socio-behavioural rootedness, which concerns integration into formal and informal social networks and the community. The third is an "autobiographical insideness", or a repository of memories, providing a sense of identity, continuation of one's life trajectory. This relates to the past, present and future. The fourth is a passive belonging, or an instrumental form of belonging relating to access to jobs, social entitlements and benefits. The fifth is governmental belonging, or ownership and control over national affairs and the nation's destiny in terms of citizens who get involved, engaged and contribute to society.

The overall score of Singaporeans on the rootedness scale in this survey was 74 out of a maximum of 100. While 74 appears to be quite a decent figure, there is no equivalent benchmark, and thus there is no means by which this result can be compared across countries apart from us conducting the survey again over time. In a comparison of the data across the different ethnic groups, 31 percent of Indians and 14 percent of Chinese had a high score for rootedness (see Table 1). 24 percent of seniors aged 60 to 64 had a high score for rootedness, but 14 percent and 18 percent respectively of the younger age groups of adults aged 30 to 44 and 15 to 29 had a high score for rootedness. A surprising finding was that 21 percent of Working Class respondents (skilled, semi-skilled and unskilled workers) and 13 percent of the Service Class (managers, professionals and associate professionals) scored well on rootedness. 21 percent of survey respondents thought that the government was doing a good job, while none (0 percent) thought that the government was doing badly. It appears that good government performance helps to bring about rootedness. 23 percent of respondents with a high degree of social capital (defined as the extent to which one could count on the support of, as well as be counted upon by one's social networks to provide support) scored high on the rootedness scale while only 16 percent of those with low degree of social capital scored highly on the rootedness scale. People who demonstrated a high degree of social capital tended to be very connected within their neighbour-hood, and exhibited a high degree of trust and reciprocity amongst friends and family members.

Table 1 Selected subgroups in the IPS Survey on Rootedness

The numbers in parenthesis are the percentage of the subgroup that scored well in rootedness.

Overall Score = 74/100	
Indians (31%)	Chinese (14%)
Seniors 60–64 (24%)	Adults 30–44 (14%) Young 15–29 (18%)
Working Class (21%)	Service Class (13%)
High Evaluation of Governmental Performance (21%)	Low Evaluation of Governmental Performance (0%)
High Social Capital (23%)	Low Social Capital (16%)

HOW CAN WE DEVELOP ROOTEDNESS?

The following are some hypotheses on barriers and facilitators to the development of rootedness. First, the over-emphasis on meritocracy and self-reliance has sent out the message that Singaporeans need to depend on themselves. While there is some degree of welfarism in Singapore in the sense of government subsidies and cash hand-outs for the poorest, there is a greater sense that Singaporeans are on their own. This is not conducive for the cultivation of rootedness. Perhaps a more balanced approach is needed here.

Second, although it is said in the domain of public rhetoric that "Every Singaporean Matters", there is much emphasis on market relations in reality. This tends to convey the message that the economic value-add of Singaporeans matters more than their membership as citizens.

Third, which I have mentioned above, is the lack of a culture of affirmation and a broader definition of success and contribution. The way I see it, only qualifications, net worth, and being world-class matters in Singapore. In reality, only the top 5 percent to 10 percent of the population will qualify as world-class at most. What will then happen to the rest? Unfortunately this disparity does not stand at a 50-50 divide, but we are instead likely to see 90 percent of Singaporeans in the lower end, and 10 percent who qualify as world class. So I think we need a culture of affirmation and a broader definition of success and contribution.

Fourth, is Singapore more of an economy or a nation? We have to start thinking of ourselves as a nation and a community. Conceiving of ourselves as an economy is not conducive to the development of rootedness.

Fifth, is there a tolerance of differences, or the acceptance of people with different ideas, viewpoints and paradigms? My sense here in Singapore is that very often we cannot let our hair down, and always have to look over our shoulder. We would, if we are among friends and fellow members in the community, be able to relax and speak our minds freely.

Having said all this, all is not lost. The process of enhancing rootedness has already begun in earnest. The government has demonstrated through S21 and National Education that it has identified what needs to be done to encourage Singaporeans to think of Singapore as a nation, and we need to facilitate the process of Singaporeans thinking of Singapore as a nation.

WHERE ARE WE HEADING?

So where are we heading? Is globalisation a threat to rootedness? In my view, globalisation has nudged Singaporeans to make a choice of asking themselves "Is Singapore my home, wherever I may be?" Geographical mobility "forces" Singaporeans to make comparisons and hopefully with this, Singaporeans will decide that Singapore is still home where they find acceptance and security. On the issue of the influx of foreign talent, my feeling is that Singaporeans will demonstrate a generosity of spirit towards new citizens, PRs and foreigners if and when they feel secure, accepted, and affirmed in their own country.

7

The "Problem" of Rootedness: An Emperor's Narrative?

ELEANOR WONG

INTRODUCTION

When I was invited to speak on this topic, I racked my brains as to why I would even be asked to comment in this area. It is not within my academic research or expertise. Nor is it an area in which I have fresh empirical information to share. Fortunately, on those scores, the other speaker on this panel has more than made up for my inadequacies. So, I finally came to the conclusion that I might have been invited because, in my "sideline" as a playwright, I am permitted to indulge in flights of fancy and thus to contribute a different, unexpected, outlier perspective. And such a perspective, however frivolous, might have some small space in a conference on Singapore Perspectives.

I will thus start with a point that might reflect a personal prejudice as a writer: facts are not "real" until we embed them into some sort of narrative. The story or the perspective from which we look at facts colours our view on any given issue. Take the topic of rootedness. In our national discussions, rootedness (or its supposed lack) is often framed as a matter for concern or worry. This problematising of rootedness seems to assume a narrative about nationhood and country that requires citizenship to be a lifetime commitment. (These days I am not sure that even people in love expect that.) This standard narrative also seems to require that commitment to be worked out within some physical, geographical perimeter.

But, I ask myself, is that the only satisfying narrative? Whose narrative does that feel most like?

So the second point I want to throw out, perhaps a little provocatively, is that the "problem" of rootedness implied in the standard narrative is mostly an "Emperor's Story". The only story that requires rooted citizens for a long period is the story of the king. The story of the king is meaningless without subjects to rule over, to look after benevolently, to fuss about, to love, and from whom to receive homage and taxes. I might be cruel here and I can, as a playwright, hide behind a total lack of objectivity but let me just throw this out: maybe this story resonates most with those who are emperors or rulers, which is why they are rightly stressed-out about it, especially when the external circumstances suggest that the "ground" might want to "leave".

To test this idea, it may be interesting to look at timing, at when the national discussion on rootedness seems to take on special significance. Could the timing correspond to moments when the "Emperor" was concerned that "his" people were tempted to "escape"? For example, I think there was some discussion on rootedness in Parliament recently, about the time when financial troubles were looming globally. And previously, when then-Prime Minister Goh Chok Tong talked about "quitters and stayers", the economic circumstances were also not at their best. The potential for sad endings (in the "Emperor's Story") if the people become disaffected, disconnected and dislocated is brought into sharp focus for the political leadership at such times. Thus it is no surprise that those are the times the political leadership tends to talk about rootedness the most.

But, and this is my third point today: the "Emperor's Story" is not the only story. There are alternative stories. Stories that even the "Emperor" trots out depending on the purpose at hand. There is the alternative story of globalisation, which the "Emperor" likes to tell most of the time, because that story has a lot to do with how we make money and bring all the "goodies" in: the galleons with the gold, on which the taxes can be levied. The globalisation story is to some extent at variance with the story of rootedness and the emperor and his subjects. Because in the globali-sation story, if you are, say, Leonardo DiCaprio on the Titanic desiring to go to the new world, not wanting to be stuck where you are, it is actually a good thing. Indeed in that sub-category of emperor stories where the emperor can aspire to an empire beyond immediate geographical boundaries, rootedness is also not necessarily a good thing. The British would have been happy that many of their citizens were willing to uproot from Britain and come to malaria-infested places like Singapore to extend their empire.

In fairness to our local "Emperor", the standard "Emperor's Story" is, of course, one that has become quite attached to familiar notions of state or nation. I am not suggesting that we should discard it entirely as a tool for understanding ourselves. What I am suggesting is two-fold. First, that individual citizens (subjects) inevitably will have personal narratives and some of such narratives may legitimately require the citizen to act in ways that go against the standard idea of rootedness. When that happens, I am suggesting that there is nothing for the citizen to regret and, for the emperor, little to be gained in pushing that citizen further away by casting aspersions on his or her loyalty to the country. Second, I believe that there are other alternative narratives that may better resonate with Singaporeans today; narratives that take some of Singapore's unique characteristics into account and that also take into account changes occurring everywhere in the world.

I will attempt to spin one of those alternative narratives for consideration — that of the city.

THE COMBINED NARRATIVE LENS OF THE CITY AND "TENANCY"

The narrative of the city, as opposed to the standard narrative of state, is an alternative narrative that resonates with me. It accounts for some innate characteristics that differentiate Singapore from states that have extensive hinterlands and large physical perimeters.

I lived and worked in New York City for several years. New York has a core of "native" New Yorkers. But it is a small core. By far the majority of my colleagues, for example, had come to New York seeking careers, but intending once the children came, to move out, at the very least across the river, to upstate New York, or to New Jersey; any place where the kids could run in the backyard. Some aspired to second careers back in their home states or further afield. Yet New York works and New Yorkers (whether native or transplanted) are proud of their association with the city, even years after they have long left. Loyalty or contribution to a city may not require permanent physical adherence. The city can function as a stage in a journey or a stepping stone. The city often receives a person's most vigorous and productive years. There is no shame in being a city.

From the perspective of the narrative of the city, Singapore has done quite well. Most of us do not leave the moment the children come. Of those who do leave, many see emigration as an option for when they are really old and want to lounge on the veranda and sip tea or alcohol, or whatever makes them feel better about their lives at that point. For these people, peace and tranquillity may not be optimal in an urban setting. Or they may want to regularly indulge in activities that, by definition, cannot be provided by a small island like Singapore. These days, some retire young and go skiing or cycling around the world. As a country that cannot provide many of these amenities, Singapore should thus expect some attrition emigration and should be happy that by far the majority do not leave, despite these lifestyle considerations. In any event, there is a point beyond which the idea that "home is where one returns at the end of the day" fails, as any workaholic's spouse will testify to.

The narrative of the city (or the stepping stone) also accounts for changes in mobility and pace that, I believe, will increasingly affect the concept of citizenship for all countries, not just an island-state like Singapore.

Let me introduce this point with an obvious observation. Where you start and end a story makes a lot of difference. The act of meeting someone, whom you then fall in love with, is often posited as the start of a lovely romance. If the story is cut off at the walk down the aisle, you indeed get a happy romance. If we cut the same narrative off 20 years later, it might veer into a less rosy genre! That is, the timeframe we choose affects the nature of the narrative.

The current discussions and concepts of citizenship suggest that our timeframe has to be quite long; basically our whole lives (and possibly generations of families). This made a lot of sense when persons had no choice but to live and die where they were born. This timeframe may still make sense in some contexts (think apple pie and picket fences). However, my own sense is that we are long past that sort of world, for better or worse. Changes in technology, the pace of life and the speed at which we can travel and communicate with each other: all these mean that many significant projects in our lives can be completed in a much shorter timeframe. If we plug these factors into the plot mix, then even more we get a narrative that is multi-stage (much like the city narrative), where citizenship, commitment or rootedness to any single place is better described as a medium-term tenancy rather than a perpetual fee simple, one that is held forever. A more appropriate timeframe by which to measure commitment or belonging in these changed circumstances might be 10 or 20 (adult?) years, perhaps less. This timeframe is enough for a good story to be told, and for us to be quite happy with it, which might then be all we should require of someone's rootedness[1].

The combined narrative of a tenancy and city resonates with me. But it is not just a subjective matter. If this narrative more appropriately "fits" Singapore today, then there are practical consequences. For example, it may suggest that we should re-think where to draw the line between those whom we consider part of our core community (include anyone prepared to spend at least ten years here); it may tip the issue of dual citizenship into an easy no-brainer; it may suggest that we should be more "worried" about "losing" members of our adult workforce to overseas careers than about bidding farewell to our overseas retirees[2]. Certainly, it suggests that some

---

[1] One comment that came up several times during the question-and-answer session was why I did not include a love story as one of my alternative narratives. I should make it clear that my preferred narrative of city-tenancy does not at all preclude love, and that I would very much like the story of my relationship with my chosen community/leaders to be one of love (including within it those crucial elements of mutual trust and respect). But, even taking the love story analogy at face value, my view is that if we allow ourselves to consider romantic love without pre-conceptions, it is possible to imagine loving more than one person (or family) in one's life, to complete one project (raising one family) in 20 years and to still have time, energy and love enough for more (think of spouses who lose their partners early in life). Indeed, and here I will no doubt offend some readers, if we were not socialised into a concept of monogamous, life-long romantic love, we might accept that love relationships are equally capable of being analysed as long-term tenancies rather than fee simples.

[2] As the reader can probably tell from the general tone of this paper, I would not personally consider this last distinction (between career stage and retirement stage) a matter for concern (hence the quotation marks around "worry" and "losing").

actions (e.g., eventually retiring to a different country) that might be viewed as "problems" under the standard view of rootedness are not really that big of a deal. New York City does not begrudge Florida its retirees.

More personally, it means that I need not feel bad when my prime minister stands up there and scolds me for wanting to move on from Singapore at some point in my life. I can feel that I have done my bit for that tenancy period that I was here, and for the projects that this country rightly called upon me to perform. I can be happy with the country and love it for a period. After that, I may well love another somewhere else.

THE "PROBLEM" OF ROOTEDNESS AND OTHER COMMON NARRATIVES

I have been making the point that how one views the "problem" of rootedness depends on one's dominant narrative. It must immediately be clear that there are many different narratives. And this brings me to my final (biggish) point: at the end of the day, human beings, not nations, spin the narratives.

When it comes to spinning the narratives of any political community (e.g., a narrative of a state), the main groups of storytellers are presumably the governors and the governed. I have suggested that the standard narrative is an "Emperor's Story" and thus more likely to suit the governors. I have also suggested that, when talking of rootedness, the city-tenancy narrative might resonate today (and might thus have a good chance of being accepted by both governed and governors as a dominant narrative). In this last section, I would like to run through some issues that often come up in the context of rootedness and consider how they might be viewed differently depending on who is telling the story and what story they are telling. (Table 1 summarises the three issues and the varying responses.)

The first "issue" is the conflict that is often supposed between the standard story of rootedness (loyal, altruistic, willing to die for nation) and materialism (self-centred, opportunistic). Here, the government arguably contributes to the confusion because, as mentioned earlier, at different times it spins narratives that alternately emphasise/encourage both extremes of this supposed dichotomy. When we discuss rootedness, we bemoan the people's so-called over-emphasis on materialism. However, the governors themselves often spin Singapore's story as one that is all about how much of an investment this place is worth. They speak of treating our homes as investments. Well, if one talks in those terms, then obviously the smart move is to sell if there is any risk to the value; indeed, the investment story requires that one sell out in order to realise one's gains.

The second "issue" is that of our system of governance. The information suggests that some persons who leave Singapore do so because they disagree with the way Singapore is governed. At the risk of overgeneralisation, the leavers usually prefer a more inclusive system. Some believe that if Singapore had a more "democratic" system, the current government would be removed from power and blame the fact that this has yet to occur on Singapore's lack of freedom. On this issue, once we understand the dominant narratives of the three relevant story-telling groups, the whole story fits together quite coherently. The *government's* narrative has been clear and consistent throughout: it has instituted a system of rule-by-elite. This narrative tries to incorporate those of us who have proven to be both capable and willing to brown-nose[3] into some part of that elite, and also suggests that citizens should trust this elite because it delivers the goods. From the perspective of the *governed*, most of the citizenry will find that this is quite a satisfying and happy story as long as the government delivers. This should come as no surprise. Most people do not mind a story where someone else takes care of them. Who then would find a closed, elite system frustrating? If I might suggest — a *putative governor*, a citizen who thinks that he is capable enough to be part of the elite but disagrees with and has thus been excluded from the ruling elite. Unfortunately, in an elite

---

[3] The term may seem pejorative but is used in humour and I would be the first to confess that I am not immune from the temptations of flattery and inclusion into some inner sanctum (even at a fairly outer ring). Putting this more seriously (and acknowledging the complexity of the issue), some of us may not agree with everything our government does but may nonetheless feel that we can contribute to the national project at different levels of remove, while retaining our integrity and independence.

Table 1 Dominant narratives can actually lend a clue to why some people choose to leave

The Governor's Versus The People's Perspectives On Three Issues

Issue	Governor's Perspective(s)	People's Perspective(s)	EW's Comments
Standard Rootedness vs. Opportunistic Materialism	Mixed signals. Sometimes the "Emperor's Story" dominates. Sometimes the Corporate/Globalisation story dominates	At the crunch, if there is a disjunct between individual material survival and the survival of a construct such as the state, people are almost certain to choose personal (or immediate community) survival. There can be no personal story if the narrator dies.	The standard "Emperor's Story" can be seen as a powerful myth that sometimes succeeds in overcoming the natural human tendency to prefer self-survival. Emperors who manage to convince their subjects of this myth forge a strong "national spirit". A variant that works quite well because it taps into a person's natural association with his/her immediate group is the military stalwart: "Die for your buddies." In Singapore, the mixed signals of the government exacerbate the conflict and arguably favour the selfish, materialistic response.
System of Government	Rule by Elite	For most people, their narrative need not include a huge element of self-government as long as they enjoy some minimum liberties and the elite deliver.	Putative governors who disagree with the elite will either have to find a means to contribute with integrity or will find this system constraining/frustrating and, possibly, leave. For those who leave, there is very little point in persuading them to stay because (as long as they see themselves as having no honest place in the elite) there is no incentive.
Foreign Talent	The "Emperor's Story" naturally prefers a clean, distinct line between legal citizens and "foreigners". It also views certain groups of "foreign talent" as more transitory than others. It is natural for governors to think of their subjects as units of investment and return (as assets and burdens) and thus to want to draw the line at allowing potential "burdens" in.	The people's story has two major themes. The first theme focuses on our shared lives with foreign talent (place of origin should have little impact on our actual activities and interactions). The second theme is one of "fear of the different"; this theme supports attitudes of ethnic, racial, social distinction/separation.	Here, the conflicting stories come on the people's side. Fear of the different coupled with the "Emperor's Story" will support a dominant attitude that the foreign talent issue is a "problem" for rootedness. But if the governors are willing to take a risk on a more creative narrative (e.g., city-tenancy) and can tap into the competing human story of shared lives, foreign talent becomes a pool of potential rootedness that can support nation-building (as demonstrated by Singapore's history).

system, this citizen is going to leave because there is no incentive to stay on. You might as well just let him go[4]. The foregoing analysis dovetails with Ern Ser's statistics to some extent. Ern Ser was surprised that those in the category of the Working Class appear to be more rooted than those in the Service Class. I am less surprised. The government has quite successfully told the story of "rule-by-elite" and, more importantly, it has delivered to some extent. So, it is not surprising that, for the Working Class, this is an acceptable plot.

Foreign talent is another "issue" that has often been brought up in the context of rootedness. It is usually presented as a problem of assimilation, dilution, competition with the so-called native population. I think the standard "Emperor's Story" requires the government to place a divide between citizenship and non-citizenship (and that this divide is actually not helpful for the community). As I said earlier, the "Emperor's Story" is predicated upon the existence of subjects. The only way for you to distinguish the "subject" is with some kind of label. A label that differentiates the subject, who is required (often by law) to obey the emperor, from the foreigner who is not required to[5]. In Singapore, the government's foreign talent narrative has a further distinction. There's a divide, a line separating "us and them", between citizens and *two* groups of foreigners. One group is portrayed as coming in at the top to provide all the "brain stuff" that we may not have enough of. Another group is portrayed as coming in at the bottom to provide all that "muscle stuff" to do what we do not want to do. With that second group, the story — and legal — line is clearly drawn that they are foreigners, who are temporarily here, so that there is no chance these people will ever become part of our

---

[4] A classic multi-party democratic system accommodates many more putative governors with different views because it holds out the possibility that, at different intervals, different groups of governors will be in power. Some of us might think that this is a good thing (to retain the services of more putative governors) but, my simple point in this paper is merely that IF one accepts the dominant narratives in today's Singapore, one must expect some putative governors to walk away.

[5] In fairness to Singapore, this is the current label that is adopted by nations all around the world (with minor variations). It would admittedly take a fairly radical change of perspective (perhaps to a city-tenancy model as I have suggested) and some creative legal thinking to adopt a model that departs from this standard view.

community. With the first group, the fence is slightly more porous; permanent residency is an option.

I suggest that while these divisions seem crucial from a government perspective, they are not necessary, or even beneficial, if we tell the foreign talent story from the standpoint of a community of human beings working and living with each other. Those who come to live and work with us, perhaps as our domestic assistants, perhaps as our managers, surely do not need to be treated as outsiders. In fact, the view that these foreign talent (in both categories) are simply people whom we live and work with, is more conducive to long-term assimilation, rootedness and belonging. This is, of course, self-evident in any *Mediacorp* historical serial in every scene of our forebears arriving on boats, working in menial positions. We view this story, 40 years on, as that of our roots, even as our current foreign talent story denies others the possibility of rootedness. Especially if you accept my idea of a city-tenancy narrative, it becomes clear that the citizenship distinctions that the "Emperor's Story" may draw are, to some extent, artificial. If people come with the expectation and the hope that at some point they can be part of this community, assimilation and rootedness are much more likely to take place.

CONCLUSION

At the end of the day, we will live our lives according to the narratives that resonate, that are authentic, that are not imposed on us (and governors will do better, I reckon, in convincing their subjects to play along with their narratives if they choose narratives that better resonate with those subjects).

Ironically, however, I find myself facing the rather paradoxical conclusion that I might not mind that my Emperor believes in the "Emperor's Story". That belief makes my Emperor somewhat stressed about whether I am happy, makes my Emperor worry if I want to leave, prods my Emperor into coming up with initiatives like S21. Now, as long as *I* am not stressed out by this, as long as *I* know that there are other stories out there that are equally valid, stories by which I can lead a principled and happy and valuable life, then maybe I do not quite mind that my Emperor minds. Perhaps, it is not that bad a bargain to make.

SECTION **IV**

Can Singapore Preserve Its Hub Status?

CHAPTER 8

Can Singapore Preserve Its Hub Status?

TAN KIM SONG

The topic, "Can Singapore Preserve its Hub Status", is one that is close to the hearts of many people. The word "hub" is of course not new to Singapore. Having begun as a regional trading port, Singapore's economic history before independence was largely a record of its position as a regional trading and commercial hub. This is not surprising. As a small economy with hardly any natural resources, strategic geographical location is probably the only real natural competitive advantage Singapore had. Industries that flourished during Singapore's early years were industries that benefited directly from Singapore's strategic locality.

Since 1965, the Singapore government has been very aggressive in trying to broaden and redefine Singapore's competitive advantage. Building on Singapore's strategic location, the government has added to the list of factors that make Singapore attractive, as a place to do business. These include political stability, human capital, good physical infrastructure, organisational software and efficiency. It has also engaged in various forms of strategic industrial policy, aimed at identifying and encouraging the growth of certain industries that are seen to be "winners", thereafter making Singapore a hub of those industries.

From an economist's point of view, there has always been the age-old question of how a hub should evolve. Should it be left to the private sector? To free market forces? Or should it be government-led? In Singapore's case, our hub status in a number of industries is very much a result of strong government initiatives, supported by a wide range of resources.

Yet, in recent years, we have also seen that it is not difficult for other countries in the region to emulate or even duplicate some of the key ingredients that make Singapore a hub city: physical infrastructure, good governance and organisational efficiency. Even an advantage as unique as strategic geographical location may not as permanent as we thought. Hence the question: can Singapore preserve its hub status?

In the session this afternoon, I hope that the speakers will help us understand and answer two questions. Firstly, what does being a hub mean for Singapore and what kind of hub are we aiming to be? It would be particularly useful if the speakers could help shed some light on the criteria policy makers use in deciding what kind of hub Singapore should be.

The second question is: what should Singapore do going into the future? Should it follow the same strategies as before, or are new strategies needed because the world has changed so much? In particular, it would be good if the speakers can discuss how the current global economic crisis might affect Singapore's hub status.

CHAPTER 9

Reinventing Singapore: Global City — From Host to Home

TAN CHIN NAM

As I am no longer involved directly in the economic development function in the civil service, in preparing for this presentation I organised a breakfast meeting with the CEOs of three statutory boards, namely, the Economic Development Board (EDB), International Enterprise Singapore (IE Singapore) and the Singapore Tourism Board (STB), all of whom were with me at the EDB when I was its Managing Director. In the course of discussing how Singapore should be a hub or otherwise, I was very much intrigued by the comments made by EDB's Managing Director. He said that right now the EDB is focusing on how to transit companies from treating Singapore as a host to making it a home.

That set me rethinking about the topic I was supposed to address: Can Singapore preserve its hub status? I actually do not quite like the term "hub" as it is quite a threatening idea in the sense that if we are the hub, then the others are the less important spokes. It is not a "win-win" situation. I would rather have a more neutral way of describing Singapore's role, for instance, as a "city", a "capital", or even a "centre". My presentation therefore shall focus on Singapore's changing role as a global city.

During this morning's proceedings, quite a bit was discussed about how Singaporeans should be engaged, and how we should also be involved in making this a happy society. In response to that, I shall not only adopt an economic perspective to look at things in my presentation. Although economics will be a predominant focus and my natural bias, I would like to comment on how we can evolve Singapore into a better place for people to live, work, play and learn as a global city.

Right now, with the financial crisis, we are all immersed in a very critical situation. Every day, we read about more and more bad news. But, Singaporeans should not lose heart. We must of course do our best to manage the present and yet at the same time create the future. After all, Singapore has gone through 45 years of economic transformation, which has brought us to where we are today. Hence, I would like to start off by first re-examining the idea of a "hub".

In 1986, when I was posted to the EDB to participate in the repositioning of the economy, we adopted a new strategic vision of Singapore as a global city with total business capabilities. Why total business capabilities? Because the Economic Committee set up in 1985 to deal with Singapore's first recession after independence recommended that Singapore must embrace the services sector and not just the manufacturing sector for a more balanced growth. This became the core tenet of how EDB would reinvent itself. We then adopted this positioning of Singapore as a global city with total business capabilities. By adopting a multi-agency approach, Singapore agencies all embraced this repositioning. In fact, over the next 20 to 30 years or so, we would see hubs everywhere. Practically every agency or ministry in Singapore would have its version of positioning Singapore as a global hub in its own functional area. Our agencies are quite connected. This collective vision is frequently exhibited in a whole array of reinforcing themes adopted for our National Day Parades over the years, a reflection of unity of purpose.

However, in looking at how Singapore has evolved to become a global hub, or a global city, not many people realise that apart from Singapore's ability to host companies, we already had our global city vision many years ago. In fact, Mr S. Rajaratnam, Singapore's first Foreign Affairs Minister, first coined the concept of Singapore as a "global city" in 1972. When he delivered a speech to the Singapore Press Club, he articulated his vision of how Singapore should be interlinked with the rest of the world as a global city. The external dimension was thus very clearly expressed. However, if you were to go into the Internet now, search for "global city" using Google, chances are you will find many entries that suggest Professor Saskia Sassen was the first to coin the term in 1991. In actual fact, it was Mr Rajaratnam who coined the term in 1972, and that has been how Singapore adopted this external perspective in developing itself to become a global city.

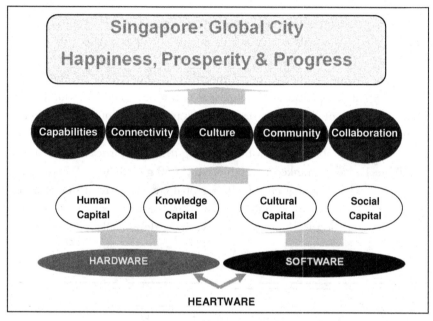

Figure 1 How Singapore should evolve as a global city

HOW SINGAPORE CAN BECOME A GLOBAL CITIY

Figure 1 is my own perspective on how a global city could evolve. What I call "heartware" must be addressed first. Heartware addresses how we want to develop a country and encompasses both the hardware and software aspects. Some would even call it "soulware". This must embrace human capital, knowledge capital, cultural capital and social capital, or citizen engagement. Hence, I have five Cs describing how a global city could evolve:

- Capability;
- Connectivity, which would include telecommunication and ICT (information and communication technology);

– Culture;
– Community, that is, community development and how we can be a welcoming community towards new talent, as well as in helping people remain rooted to Singapore; and
– Collaboration

This is my paradigm with regards to how Singapore could evolve to become a global city. I have also included happiness, prosperity and progress as elements of the paradigm. For Singaporeans, when we go to school, we recite the Singapore Pledge every morning at the school assembly. We declare happiness, prosperity and progress for our nation in our pledge which was incidentally also crafted by Mr Rajaratnam. This should remain as our goal as we transit and evolve Singapore to become a global city.

So, are we a global city or not? According to A.T. Kearney's latest survey (see Table 1), we are ranked seventh amongst 60 global cities. We are thus, already viewed as a global city. To be a global city, you have to be a leader in aspects of business, human capital, information exchange, cultural experience, and political engagement. We have done well in the business

Table 1 The 2008 Global Cities Index

Ranking	City	Business Activity	Human Capital	Information Exchange	Cultural Experience	Political Engagement
1	New York	1	1	4	3	2
2	London	4	2	3	1	5
3	Paris	3	11	1	2	4
4	Tokyo	2	6	7	7	6
5	Hong Kong	5	5	6	26	40
6	Los Angeles	15	4	11	5	17
7	Singapore	6	7	15	37	16
8	Chicago	12	3	24	20	20
9	Seoul	7	35	5	10	19
10	Toronto	26	10	18	4	24

Source: Foreign Policy and a survey conducted by A.T. Kearney, and The Chicago Council on Global Affairs

activity aspect, but perhaps more can be done in the cultural experience aspect. I think the survey is quite insightful. It points to a certain direction in regards to how to evolve Singapore further.

I have reinterpreted EDB's economic development curve into this particular formulation (refer to Figure 2). Over the last 40 to 50 years, we have evolved from a labour-intensive phase to one that is skills-intensive, capital-intensive, and finally, knowledge-intensive. In the future, we will have to become innovation-intensive and experience-intensive, in other words we will need to have a creative economy. This has tremendous implications in terms of how we want to move up the economic ladder. What sort of capabilities do we need? What sort of connectivity do we need in order to realise this new version of our global city positioning?

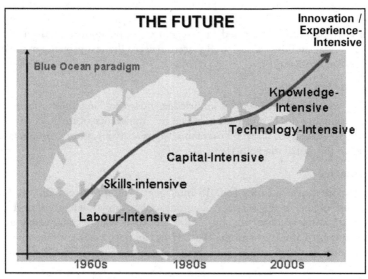

Source: EDB

Figure 2 Singapore's development path

The Economic Review Committee in 2003 formulated a new direction for Singapore as a globalised, entrepreneurial, and diversified economy with manufacturing and services as the twin engines of growth.

Subsequent strategic development within the public sector adopting Blue Ocean Strategy (BOS) thinking came up with a new growth formula for Singapore: World • Singapore. This is a new articulation of Singapore Unlimited, with the world in Singapore and Singapore in the world, emphasising the four attributes of Singapore: Trust, Knowledge, Connected and Life. Refer to Table 2. After all, our aspiration is to build on our trusted role as a global business city to become a knowledge economy, with connectedness, and also very importantly, liveability for a meaningful, happy and enriching life. By liveability, I mean being a place for people to work, live, play and learn: the integration of all four aspects.

Table 2   The four attributes of Trust, Knowledge, Connectedness and Life are essential to positioning Singapore as a global city

---

1) Trust

Is it sufficient with Singapore's reputation as a trusted business partner, and its competencies in other sectors, to move Singapore into the World space as a global city? Singapore is located in a region of opportunities at the heart of Southeast Asia, and thus we are well-placed to serve the fast-growing markets of the Asia-Pacific region.

2) Knowledge

Building an economy driven by knowledge, how can Singapore enhance the cultural capital of its hybrid nation, borne of immigrants from India to China, to create a fusion of East+West+more to place Singapore's products and services in the global marketplace?

3) Connected

As Singapore moves into the IN2015 Intelligent Nation project with interactive and digital online media services alongside online broadcasting supported by island-wide wireless networks, the entire city-state will be connected to the global capitals of the East and the West. How can businesses leverage upon this connectivity?

4) Life

As Singapore gears up for an extreme makeover across various service sectors from the launch of the Integrated Resorts to the relocation of the Marine Bay, can Singapore call itself a cool place to live, to work and play?

Moving ahead, we will therefore have to embrace the cultural aspect, the vibrancy aspect, in order to make Singapore even more attractive. I have two quotations here, one from Prime Minister Lee Hsien Loong and one from Minister Mentor Lee Kuan Yew:

"...to stand out as a truly distinctive global city, Singapore cannot be just an economic marketplace. We must also create a living environment that is the best in Asia — a city rich in culture, that exudes our own Singaporean brand of diversity and vibrancy."

Prime Minister Lee Hsien Loong at the official opening of
the new Peranakan Museum,
25 April 2008

"The old model on which I worked was to create a First World City in a Third World region — clean, green, efficient... These virtues are no longer sufficient. Now we have to be an economically vibrant and exciting city to visit, with top class symphony orchestras, concerts, drama, plays, artists and singers and popular entertainment... We have to develop our high culture — symphony orchestra, ballet, the arts... We must also develop our popular culture — pop singers, TV dramas... This is today's global village that we have to be a part of...Singapore has got to reposition itself in this world."

Minister Mentor Lee Kuan Yew, Parliament speech,
19 April 2005

Richard Florida, who created the term "creative class", examined the rise of creative people comprising artists, knowledge workers, bankers, lawyers in cities with vibrancy and growth potential. The creative class requires an environment to nurture creativity and innovation. If the city does not have the capacity to generate that kind of eco-system, then we will have a flight of the creative class. In his latest book, he asks: Who is your city?[1] What sort of city do you have? How are you linked to the mega-region so that

---

[1] In Richard Florida's book *Who's your city?*, Florida illustrated the increasing clustering of population, innovation and higher-level economy activity in only a handful of locations, which he describes as "mega-regions". Examples of mega-regions include Greater Tokyo, the Boston-New York-Washington corridor and the Chicago-Pittsburgh mega-region.

you will be able to have a congregation of creative talent for knowledge workers to add a lot of value in the city's transformation, positioning and repositioning? Thus, this kind of formulation is quite interesting because he also talks about "place happiness". Talent is attracted to and retained in a place where people can find expression, happiness and engagement. If we were to link this back to the Singapore Pledge of happiness, prosperity and progress for our nation, are we there yet? What else has to be done? This has to be the focus of the discussion this morning.

THE IMPORTANCE OF COLLABORATION

In Minister Mentor Lee's recent visit to Nanyang Polytechnic, he suggested Singapore will have to embrace diversity much more henceforth. After all, in the next phase of development, everyone is a talent. This is why we have the Arts School and the Sports School[2]. Our society has been very left brain-oriented for a long time with our emphasis on logic, engineering, mathematics and science. These were obviously important in the earlier phases of our economic development as a manufacturing centre and even now as we embrace research and development in a significant manner. However, as we move forward to the next stage of development, the creative right brain must be activated in order for us to be more innovation- and creativity-intensive for new value creation. The left brain and the right brain, in fact, the whole brain will have to be working in tandem in order to be able to create the differentiation, to deliver the experience. In the next phase of development, a closer collaboration between the public and the private sector, as well as the people sector, will become necessary. That is why the fifth C in my model (refer to Figure 1) is Collaboration, and it is becoming extremely important.

---

[2] Embracing diversity is reflected at the infrastructural level. Singapore is fortunate to have committed to building its arts, sports and special schools. Nonetheless, it is important that the attitude to embrace diversity is well-internalised at the social level. In contrast to the conservative mindset of fearing to make mistakes, such an openness to diversity will also entail the need for "open-to-experience" and the courage to create ideas, success as well as failures.

Singapore's Hyflux, which is a leader in environment solutions such as water treatment, is by now a well-known company. It has entered into what is a very unique public-private partnership to create NEWater for Singapore using reverse osmosis membrane technology for desalination. Hyflux delivers projects on a design, build and operate basis. Due to this kind of public-private partnership, Hyflux is now a major player in our internationalisation drive. The company is able to secure multi-million dollar projects in many places in the world. This is thus a good illustration of the public-private partnership at work.

Another good illustration is in the area of Interactive Digital Media (IDM) initiative as part of National Research Foundation's five billion dollars allocation for additional national-level Research & Development on top of what the Agency for Science and Technology Research (A*STAR) has set out to do. Of this sum, $500 million has been allocated for IDM R&D. This is to build on our three decades of information and communication technology (ICT) development, and it has worked very well. Under the IDM Jumpstart and Mentor (iJAM) micro-financing initiative, we have $50,000 invested in each selected IDM project conceived by capable individuals. The vision is to support 1,000 new innovative projects over a five-year period. Right now, we have already supported 200. Some of these companies are still new, but because of the mentoring approach adopted, they have been able to make extremely good progress by being linked to the universities and given access to incubators. Four of these companies have already won national and international ICT awards. This illustrates that creativity can happen on the ground. But it does require a collaborative approach: tying up with the university, the private sector, and people with the ideas and know-how.

Moving forward, how can we become more attractive? How can we become a more entrepreneurial economy? A more entrepreneurial global city? In the lifestyle area, we have apparently done quite well. BreadTalk is now a household name; they also run Food Republic, food courts with a difference. George Quek, the founder of this company, actually had qualifications in design. So, he was able to use his right brain and connect it to his left brain to generate economic value. We have also seen examples from Banyan Tree, and international companies such as Aman Resorts, using Singapore as their global headquarters. We have to hone in on their expertise, make them feel comfortable in Singapore as a place to do business and expand.

In the area of architecture, I think we have also done quite well. RSP Architects has about 1,200 staff, and the owner has told me that the company is probably the second-largest in the world. They have 550 staff in India, and they have significant projects in the Middle East, Vietnam and elsewhere. DP Architects, which implemented the Esplanade Theatres by the Bay, is also doing very well in the Middle East and beyond. The Dubai Mall, the largest mall in the world, was designed by DP Architects.

In the services area, we have already done quite well. In the next phase of our development, we should also be talking about GNP (Gross National Product) development, as opposed to GDP (Gross Domestic Product). This means there has to be income generated overseas in order to enhance Singapore's global city positioning. Another very interesting company is Olam International, which is in the food ingredients business. It connects plantation gates with factory gates, offering integrated supply chain management services, including risk management and currency management. This is to help growers do their job better and give manufacturers of food products better logistics support. Olam International now has its global headquarters in Singapore. It is an $8 billion revenue company. The Chief Executive Officer is a Singapore Permanent Resident and is doing very well. Just last week, he was at the Harvard Business School providing insights to the class on the second version of the case study written on his company. So, it is a very successful example of how a company could use Singapore as a home, as a base, to carry out global business.

CONCLUSION

As we move into the next phase of our development in the midst of this economic crisis, when many companies are in trouble and being deconstructed, there is a unique opportunity for other companies or individuals with the means to pick up parts of the businesses for reintegration or reconstruction into viable, sustainable enterprises. This will require the public and private sector collaborating in a new way.

The EDB is absolutely right about our next phase of development. How can we make companies look at Singapore as a home?[3] And more importantly, how can we make Singaporeans view Singapore as a home? To sink roots, spread their wings and provide us with the linkages globally. And this is really how a global city would evolve. In the case of Singapore, this vision actually started in 1972 and the journey is still on.

---

[3] Making Singapore our home is also reiterated in one of the theme songs for National Day — 'Home' by Ms Kit Chan.

CHAPTER 10

Can Singapore Advance as a Regional Hub?

MANU BHASKARAN

I want to look at how Singapore has done as a global city, as a regional hub. The bottom-line for me is that we have done extremely well, but the challenges are proliferating, so we need to do a lot more to fill in the gaps if we are to continue succeeding in this area. Let me begin by looking at some global rankings, one of which Dr Tan Chin Nam has shown you, to take stock of where we stand and what drives that ranking. I want to look at the challenges that we are facing, the gaps that we need to fill, and in particular to focus on what is our key gap, which is the lack of scale and which might be our undoing in the future.

First of all, what am I talking of in terms of a "hub"? The global economy is increasingly a network economy that links different global cities all over the world. Each of these global cities is like a node that switches all kinds of flows, be it flows of people, capital, ideas, telecommunications or tourists. These are nodal points, and what is important is that they create a lot of value. People in such cities can generate a lot of income, and, therefore, welfare if a city succeeds in becoming and maintaining itself as a regional hub. That is what is in it for us.

WHERE SINGAPORE STANDS

Where does Singapore stand now? I want to present to you some of the results of the MasterCard Global Centers of Commerce Index, an exercise of which I was a small part. The Index was constructed to identify the 75 most influential cities around the world that drive the global economy. Essentially, these are the drivers which we think make a successful, effective and sustainable global city.

Seven evaluative dimensions were included in the consideration of what makes a worldwide centre of commerce. The first thing is that the legal and political framework must be there to give stability and certainty to businesses so that they would locate in the centre. It must be at least stable economically, otherwise if your currency is gyrating all over the place, or if you have high inflation, it is not a very attractive place at all. We need it increasingly to be a centre of knowledge-creation and also a place where information flows freely and easily. Businesses need information to make good, well-judged decisions.

We also looked at the World Bank's indices which measured the ease of doing business. How easy is it to set up a business? How easy is it — when it is painfully necessary — to retrench workers? Liveability: is it an attractive place where you want to bring a family to, is the air breathable, are the schools good, and is the crime rate low? And then there are two achievement indicators which tell you if you have already achieved 'it' as a global centre. First, have you actually generated the volume of financial activity: stock market, foreign exchange trading, bank syndication, private wealth management, *et cetera*? Second, are you generating flows of business activity? Are there operation headquarters based in your city? Are key business decisions for the region or for the world made where you are? This is what we think drives a global hub.

Singapore has done extremely well according to this metric. In the last exercise we did a few months ago, we ranked Singapore number four and as you can see (refer to Chart 1), very close to Tokyo, but well behind London or New York. If you look at the changes (refer to Table 1), we have actually been improving. We are one of the very few cities which went up in the rankings very rapidly compared to other cities.

One of the things that came out in our exercise was that the rankings are highly dynamic. We have made it as a global city, but there is no guarantee that we will remain highly-ranked forever. For instance, Amsterdam moved up a lot, and Shanghai has moved up a few notches from virtually nowhere in every year we have done this exercise. Moscow

Chart 1 Singapore does well in the 2008 MasterCard Worldwide Centers of Commerce Index

Table 2 In the 2008 ranking exercise, Singapore moved up the list by two places

Top Ten Centers of Commerce in the world, 2008

	City	WCOC Index 2008 (out of a possible 100)	Change
1	London	79.17	0
2	New York	72.77	0
3	Tokyo	66.60	0
4	Singapore	66.16	+2
5	Chicago	65.24	-1
6	Hong Kong	63.94	-1
7	Paris	63.87	+1
8	Frankfurt	62.34	-1
9	Seoul	61.83	0
10	Amsterdam	60.06	+1

and Dubai are also making their marks in their respective regions. One thing that I noticed in these changes: cities that are rising rapidly are benefiting from a surge in activity in their particular regional hinterlands. The scale of activity is clearly very important.

What else determines changes in ranking? One thing should be said from the onset: it is very difficult to dislodge the top two cities, which are London and New York. Legacy is important, and it is easy to understand why. Once critical mass assembles in a global city, the lawyers are there because the investment banks are there; the investment banks are there because the wealth is there; the wealth is there because the lawyers and all the other services are there. Everything interlocks. No single part of this interlocking system can leave without damaging its own business potential. Once you create critical mass, it is very difficult to dislodge it.

An example of that is Beirut, which amazingly continued for quite a while — into the Lebanese civil war — to be the heart of commerce in the Middle East. It was well into the civil war before Beirut lost its status as a regional hub. Critical mass, once created, is difficult to dislodge. But what we see below the top two is constant change, and therefore Singapore is at risk. We are rising now, but the challenges are clearly increasing as you can see with Shanghai and Dubai coming up. I will talk about these challenges, and then about how we can deal with them.

WINNERS AND LOSERS

First of all, there is a great opportunity because in 2007, we had a very important historical turning point. For the first time in human history, more people lived in towns than in rural areas. Urbanisation is an important trend and clearly benefits nodal points like Singapore. Another trend is that activity is increasingly concentrated, and there are winners and losers in this trend. New York and London have clearly been the winners in the last 10 years. On the other hand, Paris, Frankfurt and Boston are still very important cities but, in the case of Frankfurt, the city has lost operational headquarters and key elements of the financial sector to London despite very hard work on the part of the Frankfurt authorities. We are in a world where more and more activity tends to gravitate towards the winners. There is room only for a truly few global cities in this new economy.

So, what do we have to face in Singapore? Clearly, the rise of the Asian giants is both an opportunity as well as a risk. The risk to us is that China and India each have the sheer scale. As they start growing, their cities can gain in scale very quickly and emerge as challengers to established global hubs like Singapore. What is also interesting is that both these countries are based on civilisations going back thousands of years, and these are countries which are very proud of their heritage, and which feel that they have lost out in the last 200 years and are hence trying to make up for lost time. They have the ambition to become top again; they see it as their natural historical role. Both are liberalising (clearly China is ahead of India); both are building infrastructure (China is well ahead of India there); both are building multinational companies on their own, and as you can see, multinational companies generate huge amounts of activity and where they locate their headquarters, can help drive a particular city's growth and prospects. And unlike the rise of the previous set of challengers for us such as Korea and Taiwan, China and India have that scale that can really cause a challenge to us.

In addition to that, you have the growth of the sub-regional economic areas close at hand. One is the Greater Mekong sub-region. The Asian Development Bank (ADB) has done excellent work to promote this sub-region, encompassing Vietnam, Laos, Cambodia, Thailand and eventually Myanmar, as well as Yunnan Province in the southern part of China. There has been a rapid growth in transport links and a huge amount of deregulation that has improved customs flows among other things. This is going to benefit Bangkok as a regional hub. Bangkok is already almost as important as Singapore in terms of being an aviation hub. It is also a very important manufacturing hub in the sense that a lot of multinational companies locate the manufacturing part of their regional headquarters in Bangkok. In China, with the improved relationship between Taiwan and the mainland and increasingly economic agreements between Hong Kong and Macau on one side and China on the other side, there is an increasing integration of the Chinese economy. With Taiwan now going to encourage liberalisation, Taipei could become more of a challenge as a regional hub.

And what about our own hinterland? In a sense, I think ASEAN (the Association of Southeast Asian Nations) has been losing out. Clearly, in the wake of the 1998 economic crisis, ASEAN has been losing out. The integration of ASEAN could have created the scale of the economy that could have benefited us. Real integration, rather than rhetorical gestures, has not really come through. We have not had the level of integration that would allow ASEAN governments to scale up, and to allow goods made in one ASEAN country to be easily sold and marketed in another. We have not had the level of integration that would allow a country registered in one ASEAN country to operate easily in another. This would have benefited Singapore.

So if you look within the region, Singapore is doing extremely well now. However, the cities I have highlighted, such as Bangkok, Shanghai and Dubai are already important challengers. I think Taipei, which has not yet deregulated or liberalised its services sector, is poised to join Shanghai to become a serious challenger in the next 10 years. Mumbai has its share of problems as we have seen with the recent terror attack and with the horrendous infrastructure that you have seen, but I guarantee you, in five years' time, they will get their act together, and the infrastructure and policy regime in Mumbai will improve significantly. By which time, the scale of activity in Mumbai will be huge. So we have a lot of challenges ahead.

If we drill down to the nitty-gritty of the MasterCard Index, what are the strengths and weaknesses? (Refer to Table 2) Clearly, in terms of strengths, we are a fantastic place to do business in. The government goes all out to make it very easy to register a business and close a business. The political and legal framework, stability, legal certainty, independence of

Table 2 Singapore's strengths and weaknesses as a global city

SINGAPORE'S RANKING: PLUSES AND MINUSES

STRENGTHS	WEAKNESSES
Ease of doing business: # 1	Financial Flows: # 11
Legal/Political: # 2	Knowledge Creation & Information Flows: # 14
Business Center: # 3	Economic Volatility: # 19
	Liveability: # 40

the judiciary, commercial cases: excellent. As a business centre, in terms of the volumes of activity that gives you critical mass: again, Singapore does very, very well.

What about weaknesses? Surprisingly, in terms of financial flows, we are not ranked all that highly and I suspect that over time, our relative ranking is going to slip. In terms of the ability to create knowledge and allowing information to flow freely, which is very important if you want to go to the next level of being a global hub, we are quite weak. In terms of economic volatility, we are rather weak, surprisingly, compared to some of the other cities. In terms of liveability, of course Singapore is a very liveable city, but all things are relative, and according to various surveys we actually do not rank all that highly in this area.

If you drill down even further, what we do well in as a regional hub is in the process areas, where the government and civil servants can manage the process and regulation. We have done very well. Trouble is, we have maxed out what we can do there. There is still intensifying competition in these areas and I think it is really in the area of the hinterland that you need critical mass and so on, where things like our port, airport, and regional business capital will face more challengers. We have performed less well in financial flows, knowledge-creation and liveability as I have said. If you look more clearly, the reason for the weakness in financial flows is, the insufficient critical mass or savings actually being managed here by domestic institutions unlike in other cities. In terms of liveability, we scored very poorly on personal freedom and the quality of life is not as good as we think it might be.

So basically, the bottom-line is: we have not really made it yet. We have been lucky, I think, and in the global context of increased competition, Hong Kong, Shanghai, Mumbai and maybe Bangkok will pose a serious problem for us. In this context, there is a lot that I think we need to do, but one of the things that strike me as being very important from a policy perspective is the need to create scale. That means real regional integration so that we have the scale to generate the kind of flows that attract people to base themselves in Singapore as a hub.

I can think of a lot of things that we have to do. Clearly, the government has been doing a lot. We have been restructuring, brought in the IRs (Integrated Resorts) which have been a taboo before, and reduced taxes. We have been giving incentives; we have allowed inward migration on a scale that few other countries allow; we have attracted a lot of new manufacturing plants which are highly value-added. We have done a lot. But clearly, we are coming to a point where we are facing a capacity constraint. That showed up in the previous economic boom, in the overheating that accompanied the growth we enjoyed. Inflation rose, and costs rose. We are hitting at the constraints of growth.

When we come down to ask the question of whether we can really make it in the future as a global hub, there are a few points that emerge. For instance, most other global cities that we compete against have two airports, a major airport and a secondary airport. In fact, London has four, New York has three, and Tokyo has two. In terms of the port, we cannot just keep growing a port. There is a physical limit to the coastline and the anchorage space that we have. If we want to move beyond to the level of global cities, we need to have a much larger population. But talented people who drive a global city demand a high quality of life. However, in Singapore we do not have that option. We are very densely-packed with no real hinterland, unlike Manhattan where one could always drive to Connecticut for commuting and leisure purposes.

A PROPOSAL

I could go on and on about what we need to do, but I want to focus on the Iskandar Region, because to me, here you have, ready-made for you, what I think would be very, very good for Singapore as well as Malaysia. I think the Iskandar Region, which the Malaysians are actively pursuing, is a great opportunity for us to scale up. It is a region that wants to do business with Singapore, a region that cannot succeed — I think — without Singapore's active help, and yet will allow us to grow beyond the limits placed on our own area. Here are some data points (refer to Table 3) to make my point more convincing.

Some people worry about Iskandar being a competitor to Singapore. I do not worry about that. Without downplaying the importance of competition, the fact is in terms of the key factors of production such as land and labour, we are complementary and do not compete. In terms of the critical mass that we need, Singapore has and can offer it to the

Iskandar Region. In terms of entrepreneurship, the Malaysians have it, and Singapore has it to some extent. I think we complement each other quite well.

Table 3 Integration with Johor: The Iskandar Region and
Singapore compared

Iskandar Region: Opportunity for Singapore

	Singapore	Malaysia/IR
Area (square kilometres)	692.7	2,216.3
Population	4.5m	1.353m
GDP (USD bn)	136.9	20
Population per sq km	6,376	631.8
GDP per sq km (USD)	197.6 million	9 million
GDP per head (USD)	30,422	14,790

Essentially, what am I saying? I am saying that although we have done extremely well, we cannot rest on our laurels. If we want to go on growing with this particular strategy, I think we need to think out of the box and we need to expand the economy beyond the confines of our geographic constraints. That, to me, means seizing the opportunity of the Iskandar Region and moving more actively with Iskandar, which can then join Singapore in success.

V

Can Government Do Less, and Singaporeans Do More?

11

Can Government Do Less, and Singaporeans Do More?

MAVIS CHIONH

Our topic today requires us to consider not just the theory of governance, but also the practice of it. In the Singapore context, how much of a role should there be for the state, and how much of a role for non-state actors, or for civil society?

The panellists and I met recently to discuss the scope of our panel, and we thought that before we got on to the discussion of the practice of governance we would first go back to the reading of the theory or theories of governance. In the theoretical realm there has been a lot of discussion in recent years about rolling back the state. There are a number of new (or new-ish) theories about how the state now has less and less of a role to play in governance. Traditional concepts of public administration relied on theories such as those from Max Weber, which assumed the public to be largely uninterested in wider political engagement and participation, and also in the institutions that were thought to be essential to the issues of governance, such as the political leadership, the party and the bureaucracy. In recent years, newer theories such as the theory of New Public Management and the public value theory of the Kennedy School emerged, all of which now seek to tell us that there is more of a role for civil society to play in the area of policy-making and decision-making.

And it is funny, but when I think about this in the Singapore context, two things come to mind. The first is a letter, which was published in *The Straits Times*' Forum Page on the 16th of January. And this was a letter from a lady who had talked about how she had taken her children to East Coast Park, and her children had been very frightened by two fierce and hungry-looking cats. She went on to say how they had seen more stray cats while they were walking around East Coast Park, adding, "I would like to raise a grave concern about the stray cat situation in East Coast Park. With so many children in the area, this needs to be addressed immediately."

And this is the sort of letter that you probably see a lot of in our newspapers. Letters which write about things like stray cats, overturned rubbish bins, buses that do not come on time, trees getting chopped down, and which invariably end with the statement, "This needs to be addressed." And the assumption seems to be, "this" needs to be addressed by the government: the government has to do something.

If you think this is a novel attitude among Singaporeans, this is not so. Take another 'feline-themed' letter again from the Forum Page of *The Straits Times*, this time one going back more than 10 years. Many of you will remember that at one point MacDonald's gave away Hello Kitty dolls with its Happy Meals. Hello Kitty dolls were big collectors' items, and so long queues were forming at MacDonald's because people wanted to be the first to get the Hello Kitty dolls. Some of these queues were disorderly, there were some who were pushing and shoving, and somebody wrote in to the Forum Page of *The Straits Times* to express dismay, and said this is very bad behaviour, and the government should do something about this.

So, on the one hand you have a global discussion of how much more civic engagement there should be in the public sphere, and on the other hand in Singapore — at least at first glance — you have people writing in to the papers about stray cats and Hello Kitty and saying, the government should do something about this sort of behaviour. So, the first question I wanted to kick off with to our panellists, and perhaps to Debra because she comes from the media industry and probably has seen more of these letters and the outpourings than we have, is: when we ask in this panel "Can Government Do Less, and Singaporeans Do More"? Is that the right question? Or do we ask, as a preliminary question, are Singaporeans prepared to do more, and is the Government ready to do less?

12

Where the Government Should Not Step Back

DEBRA SOON

Let me address the issue at hand: Can the Government Do Less, and Singaporeans, More? Obviously, the answer is "yes". But does the government want to do less, do Singaporeans want to do more? This is the crux of the question.

There are some areas which I personally feel that the government should not step back and in fact should be doing more. I will give you some examples. For instance, in society, in social spheres, in education in Singapore, we are very used to a top-down, government-organised or driven approach. Education is an area which requires tremendous resources, so there is no way that the government can step back and say, "Go ahead, do what you need to do. If the private sector thinks it can run the education sector, go ahead." Obviously, the government cannot do that.

For certain areas in education, the government needs to drive, driving different academic pathways, driving creativity, driving different routes to success, driving different ideas. The government also has to be behind the idea of appreciating that young people today must be able to step up to a whole new definition of what is good for society and for us, and recognising that excellence does not have to be from achieving 10 A1s, 11 A1s or whatever kids today achieve. The government has to drive and send these signals out. The private sector can of course do the same, but at the end of the day, funding is driven by the government, and we are as a society still very driven by what the top says, fortunately or unfortunately.

Another area in the social sphere which has generated a lot of debate and which the government needs to drive is in the area of marriage and parenthood. If the government never highlighted these issues, then people will continue doing what they do. This is not quite a popular thing to say, because parenthood and marriage are personal decisions which each and every one of us as individuals has to take. But the government needs to send that signal out and to put in the resources. Whether or not it is paternity or maternity leave or baby bonus, the finances and the resources have to be put in by the government, because the private sector, the SMEs cannot possibly say that "Yes, we'll have a six-month maternity leave package" because quite frankly, there is no incentive for the private sector to do that. Why should it? It is a cost to business. In these areas, I think the government needs to drive, to do more, and to send the signals that are necessary.

The economy is another area in which the government should not be doing too much less As we all know, in a downturn like today's, if the government does not pump-prime, does not put in resources to mop up the jobs which are going to be available, if the government does not tweak rules for SMEs, implement tax breaks and incentives, who is going to do it? When the economy is doing well, we can say to the government, "Step back, allow entrepreneurship to flourish." But in times like this, when the economy is being challenged, when we are all being challenged in the global environment, the government has the resources which most of us (either SMEs or the larger companies) do not have to be able to drive and send the signals.

In the third sphere that I wanted to speak on, which is political engagement, the government probably does not want to do more, though it has some incentives to do more, to engage audiences and what people are thinking, and to have a two-way dialogue with Singaporeans. This is because in today's context and environment, the government does not have a choice. With blogging and the Internet, young people today are more exposed. Singaporeans are global, educated, travelled, much more aware. Singaporeans who are more educated and whom you want to retain so they can drive the next lap of growth and continue Singapore's success story will pack up and leave if they feel that they are not being engaged. The government in a way has no choice.

Happily, we have seen more and more engagement by the government. Also, at the same time, Singaporeans now seem more willing to be engaged. But it is only a certain portion of the population that wants that engagement, in my view. The majority of Singaporeans are more concerned with bread-and-butter issues, with what goes on in their daily lives. And as Mavis pointed out, in issues such as the stray cat problem, the rush for Hello Kitty dolls and security for children in the neighbourhood, Singaporeans are so used to the government handling every single thing for them that they feel when these issues arise they need to be pushed to somebody else.

At the same time I would like to acknowledge that there has been a growth of civil society, that there has been a growth in the number of Singaporeans who want to be engaged and do things. HOME (the Humanitarian Organisation for Migration Economics) for instance, is a group which looks into the rights of migrant workers. And more and more Singaporeans who are well-travelled and global are stepping up to the plate to do things.

But at the same time, all of these people are engaged in civic society, and this is not political engagement *per se*. And this is where I feel that, unless there is more dialogue, we are on for a collision course sooner or later. People at HOME are advocating for workers' rights, and obviously, there are some things which the government does which would be contrary to that, for foreign workers' rights, because there are certain rules put in place to prevent immigration offences. And these clashes are going to be more and more public, and more and more open as more and more Singaporeans complain to the media, write to the media, and express their views to the media.

In conclusion, I think Singaporeans deserve the government that they get. You vote for a government that you want, and when you get that government, you should be prepared to engage with that government, openly and directly, and not be afraid to put your face and your name on your view and to expect it to be challenged. Singaporeans deserve the opposition that they get. If you think that the opposition is not good enough, then Singaporeans — instead of complaining — should step up to the plate.

Most Singaporeans are cocooned in their comfort zones, and it is so much easier in life to carry on doing what you are doing, because life is comfortable here for most of us. There will be a group of people who will not be able to pay their HDB arrears or their loans and mortgages, but these people will be taken care of by the government. The rest of Singaporeans who are in professions and in jobs: we deserve what we get. If we want to be more engaged, we need to step up to the plate and do it, because nobody else will.

CHAPTER 13

Trust and Let Go

PHILIP JEYARETNAM

I am not an expert, just a practitioner... but I suppose the one advantage I have is that I can speak from some experience, so that is what I will try and do now. Maybe, before going on to some of that experience of my own engagement, I could try to answer that earlier question which Debra has posed, which was: Are people ready to step up to the plate?

THE TRIANGLE OF SUSPICION

I wanted just to identify something which holds us back, which holds Singapore back. I identify this as a triangle of suspicion. When I first thought of it yesterday, I thought "triangle of fear", but I thought that was a bit too strong... so, triangle of suspicion. The dynamic starts like this: when you have people of different backgrounds coming together and living in close proximity, there is a strong tendency to fear your neighbours. The different smells, the customs, the behaviour... So from there you have a natural desire that somebody out there will keep your neighbours in check, that they will follow the rules, and indeed beyond having rules and implementing them and enforcing them, that someone out there will mediate between different groups in society. And you get that natural dynamic where you have that enforcer who plays a mediating role, triangulates between disparate groups and kind of takes charge.

Now, the second apex in this triangle is a philosophy within the ruling party that suggests that political competition is not a good thing, and is even bad. So you then have a suspicion when people form associations, when people come together, you have a suspicion that they are going to become platforms for political dissent and competition.

This suspicion or philosophy then fuels or leads into the third apex of the triangle, which is citizens themselves becoming cautious about associating, for fear that this is considered to be a political act, and that they might find themselves being nipped in the bud. So, I think that explains a lot of the sense that when there is a problem, the citizen does not go out and form a cat patrol society but instead writes in to the forum page of the newspaper.

Obviously, real progress on this front does depend on breaking this vicious triangle. But I would suggest that it is important to do so, and it is important to do so, because I think the old mantra that Singapore was too small for people to "rock the boat" needs to be replaced by a new idea, a new sense that Singapore is too small **not** to let people row their own boats, if that is what they want to do, not to let people change mid-stream if that is what they want to do.

PRINCIPLE OR EFFICIENCY?

Let me then just pull it back to something which I have experienced. There are a number of things I could talk about, but I thought the most obvious would perhaps be the legal profession, because that is what I spend most of my time doing, and I have that experience of having been the President of the Law Society for four years from 2003 to 2007.

The legal profession is obviously a source of social capital. It is a network that strengthens society, *et cetera*, *et cetera*, and so the question of how the legal profession is regulated is an important one. I just want to draw out from the experience of the profession the importance of considering principle as well as considering effectiveness. Sometimes when we look at this question of whether the government can do less, and people do more, we try to answer the question only in terms of, well, which is the better way of delivering the goods? Is it more effective for kidney dialysis to be the preserve of the Ministry of Health, which is a tax-funded service, or is it better for it to be a matter for the charitable private sector? And we consider it in these terms, in terms of effectiveness rather than necessarily in terms of principle.

Now, the legal profession provides us with a clear iteration of the principle that you need 'protected space' for society to thrive. The legal profession shows this most particularly because the legal profession is the bedrock of the independence of the judiciary. It is an absolute given that Singapore requires an independent judiciary for it to succeed economically. But perhaps what has not always been appreciated so clearly, and one of the things I had to spend a lot of time articulating as President was that an independent judiciary depends on an independent legal profession. When you regulate the profession you have to make sure you are not undermining or reducing that independence. There may be lots of laudable efficiency goals. You may think it is faster to regulate centrally by government, but you lose something very valuable, which is that you cannot have an independent judiciary without an independent profession, without people knowing they can be represented fearlessly by lawyers even when they are up against the state.

Let me just say that the Law Society is independent. Nobody gives instructions to anyone in the Council about what to do. But unfortunately — perhaps because of history — there is an impression that might linger and that makes it harder for the Law Society to meet its full potential, and for the legal profession to meet its full potential, because of changes that took place in the past. In particular, in the 1980s there was a serious misstep in my opinion. First of all, the Minister for Law was given the power to appoint three out of the Society's 20 Council members. Secondly, there were the changes to Section 38(1)(c) of the Legal Profession Act to not allow the Law Society to comment on legislation unless the changes have been submitted to it first.

I will just explain a little bit about both of those very quickly. When we talk about appointments by the Minister for Law, I am certainly not quarrelling with the tremendous quality that those appointees have, and the contributions that they have made. They have been fantastic. In fact, one should not generalise but if anything, they have been even more hardworking than some other members of Council who are already very hardworking. Second thing I should say is that in Singapore, "what you see is what you get". If the statute says the Minister has the power to appoint, that is all it means. The members of the Council who are appointed by government do not report back, and do not take instructions.

Can the profession not be left on its own to elect its leadership? Do appointments — even of a small number — made by the political executive not undermine the principle of independence of the legal profession? This is an important point. It makes it difficult for us when we interact with other Bar associations, not just those in developed nations but even in places like China, where the regional Bar associations are telling you that government appointments to their governing bodies are being reduced or eliminated, and then they wonder why we still have three appointments when we are such an advanced nation. Is it really necessary? If it is only a matter of perception, then is it not time to do away with it?

At the same time, we have to ask, why do we need Section 38(1)(c)? Section 38(1)(c) stipulates that the Law Society can only assist the government on legislation submitted to us. Well, I can understand that you do not want Bar associations entering politics. But the question really is, who should be deciding where the boundaries are? Is this a matter for lawmakers or politicians, or is this a matter for society as a whole? Can you not actually leave it to professional associations or other non-governmental organisations (NGOs) to decide the boundaries themselves? Maybe there will be some mistakes, but probably most of the time they will get it right, and they will get to exercise power responsibly. But if you do not even provide that space, then you are actually short-changing the professions in terms of their potential.

I think we should avoid the fallacy of thinking that that funding from the state can only happen when the entity is state-controlled, and that civil society or that protected space has to be free of state funding. I think that is misconceived. Technically, taxpayers' money is taxpayers' money... when we say that is government money, I think that is actually shorthand for taxpayers' money. And who are the taxpayers? The entire society, including civil society. What the state has, of course, is that power of raising funds from the population at large. So I think there is no contradiction in private initiatives getting public funding, and obviously in the situation of the arts, it is essential... you actually must take that position, that the arts will both be free and receive some degree of state support. The two things actually go hand-in-hand.

But I do understand the underbelly of that, which is the fear of the lack of accountability, and therefore the need to keep an eye on where the money is going, if you are funding something. But again, I would answer that by saying it is not quite right to say that all accountability is via government, via the state. People can hold associations to account directly, and there is also the role of the media. The media has played this role effectively to date: in Singapore notably in the last few years, for example, the National Kidney Foundation has been held to account.

BUILDING TRUST AND PARTNERSHIPS

As I pointed out in my introduction, we are the last man standing, we are the last independently regulated profession in Singapore. Let me just end with this. I will give an example that might alarm some and hearten others. The Australian Law Council is, I think, a remarkable institution. This is shown in the case of Mohamed Haneef, an Indian doctor who happened to have links with, who occasionally corresponded by email with one of his cousins who was one of the July bombers in London. He was arrested in Australia. It was pure guilt by association. The Australian Law Council was first off the bat saying, this is wrong. They were proven right. That is a remarkable thing, when you have even opposition parties in Australia not seeing the rule-of-law issue so clearly, the Australia Law Council was able to move so quickly. That to me is an amazing thing, for it shows the strength and the resilience of the legal profession and what it can contribute to society.

History has proved them right, but what if they had made a mistake? Well, so what, really? But that is an example of the benefits of the protected space for professional and other associations can provide. I really think that we have reached the stage in our development where we cannot afford not to have that degree of protected space, that degree of contribution from citizens and citizens banding together. If I had to sum it up, this is an area where collectively we need to think big, not just make small changes, and build trust and partnerships, in place of suspicion.

About the
Contributors

Manu BHASKARAN is an Adjunct Senior Research Fellow at the Institute of Policy Studies. He is concurrently Partner and Member of the Board, Centennial Group Inc, a policy advisory group based in Washington DC where he heads the Group's economic research practice. Mr Bhaskaran co-leads the Institute's work in the area of economics. His major area of research interest is the Singapore economy and the policy options it faces. Prior to his current positions, Mr Bhaskaran worked for 13 years at the investment banking arm of Société Générale as its Chief Economist for Asia. He began his professional career at Singapore's Ministry of Defence, where he focused on regional security and strategic issues. Mr Bhaskaran graduated from Cambridge University with a Masters of Arts and also has a Masters in Public Administration from Harvard University.

Mavis CHIONH graduated from University of Oxford in 1991 with a Bachelor of Arts in Jurisprudence and also a Masters of Law degree (2005) from the National University of Singapore. She is an officer of the Singapore Legal Service which she joined in 1991. Since joining the Legal Service, Mavis has served as a Justices' Law Clerk to the Court of Appeal, an Assistant Registrar of the Supreme Court, a Deputy Public Prosecutor in the Criminal Justice Division of the Attorney-General's Chambers, and a District Judge of the Subordinate Courts (where she headed the Civil Justice Division of the Subordinate Courts). She is currently the Deputy Principal Senior State Counsel in the Civil Division of the Attorney-General's

Chambers. The Civil Division of the Attorney-General's Chambers advises the Government of Singapore on a wide range of civil matters ranging from contract and tort matters to issues of constitutional and administrative law. State Counsel from the Civil Division also represents the Government in civil litigation matters. Outside of work, Mavis has served on the Board of the Dover Park Hospice. She is currently a director of registered charities The Trailblazer Foundation and The Kind Exchange. The Kind Exchange is an online platform that matches professionals wishing to volunteer their time and skills *pro bono* with charities and community groups in need of professional skills (http://www.thekindexchange.com). The professionals who volunteer through The Kind Exchange include lawyers, bankers, journalists, marketing professionals and IT professionals.

INDERJIT Singh is a serial entrepreneur who has founded a number of successful companies. He started his career as an engineer and left to start his own company when he was the Director of Operations of the Global Assembly and Test Operations for the Memory Division of Texas Instruments. Inderjit is also a Member of Parliament, Deputy Government Whip and the chairman of the GPCs for the Ministries of Trade & Industry and Finance. He is a board member of the Nanyang Technological University and deputy chairman of the Action Community for Entrepreneurship (ACE). Inderjit has been actively driving the transformation of the entrepreneurship landscape for start-ups and SMEs in Singapore. He authored the book *The Art and Science of Entrepreneurship*, which bridges the theory and practice of entrepreneurship. Inderjit holds a Bachelor of Engineering (Honours) degree from the Nanyang Technological University and also a Masters of Business Administration degree from the University of Strathclyde.

Philip JEYARETNAM is a partner in the law firm of Rodyk & Davidson LLP, and a Senior Counsel. In his role as President of the Law Society of Singapore from 2004 to 2007, he led the last remaining self-regulating professional body in Singapore. Aside from law, his principal interest lies in the arts, especially the literary arts. He chairs a non-profit theatre school and spent eight years on the National Arts Council. He is also the author of several fiction works, including *First Loves* and *Abraham's Promise*.

Tommy KOH is Ambassador-At-Large at the Ministry of Foreign Affairs, and Chairman of the Institute of Policy Studies and the National Heritage Board. He was formerly Dean of the Law Faculty at NUS. He has served as Singapore's Permanent Representative to the UN in New York and Ambassador to the United States of America, Canada and Mexico. He was also the President of the Third UN Conference on the Law of the Sea and chaired the Earth Summit. He was the founding Chairman of the National Arts Council and the founding Executive Director of the Asia-Europe Foundation. He has served as the UN Secretary-General's Special Envoy to Russia, Estonia, Latvia and Lithuania. He was also Singapore's Chief Negotiator for the USA-Singapore Free Trade Agreement, and has chaired two dispute panels for the World Trade Organization. Prof Koh was a member of the ASEAN Charter High-Level Task Force (HLTF) and was Chairman of the HLTF from August to November 2007.

Laurence LIEN is the Chief Executive Officer of the National Volunteer & Philanthropy Centre. Laurence previously served in the Singapore Administrative Service, rotating through different positions in the Ministries of Finance, Community Development and Sports, Home Affairs and Education. Laurence has a Bachelor of Arts from Oxford University, a Masters of Business Administration degree from the National University of Singapore, and a Masters in Public Administration from the Kennedy School of Government in Harvard University. Laurence is a Governor of Lien Foundation, Deputy Chairman of Lien Aid, board member of the Lien Centre for Social Innovation at the Singapore Management University and board member of Caritas Singapore Community Council.

ONG Keng Yong is Ambassador-At-Large in the Singapore Ministry of Foreign Affairs and Singapore's Non-Resident Ambassador to Iran. He is concurrently Director of the Institute of Policy Studies in the Lee Kuan Yew School of Public Policy at the National University of Singapore. He was Secretary-General of ASEAN (the Association of Southeast Asian Nations) from January 2003 to January 2008. His diplomatic postings have taken him to Saudi Arabia, Malaysia and the USA. He was Singapore's Ambassador to India and Nepal from 1996–1998. He was appointed Press Secretary to the Prime Minister of Singapore and concurrently held senior positions in the Ministry of Information, Communications and the Arts, and the People's Association in Singapore from 1998–2002. He is a graduate of the University of Singapore and Georgetown University (Washington DC, USA).

Peter ONG is Managing Partner for The Gallup Organization in Singapore, Hong Kong, and South-East Asia. Mr Ong joined Gallup in 2004 and was formerly from the Singapore's Prime Minister's Office and Accenture. Mr Ong has led many behavioural economics-type initiatives in both the public and private sectors. He is exceptionally interested in the concept of "Soul of the City" and its links to engaged citizenry, brain gain and a city's long-term sustainable success, and the building of successful, sustainable organisations and countries through the employment of behavioural economics approaches. Another area of deep interest for Mr Ong is Leadership Development and Transformation. Mr Ong has successfully led many initiatives in Organisational and Leadership Development for large and small enterprises, complex and simple. Mr Ong serves as a director on the boards of NVPC (the National Volunteer & Philanthropy Centre) and Gallup Singapore, Malaysia and HK. He is also an executive coach to a dozen C-suite executives leading large enterprises locally and internationally. Mr Ong earned a bachelor's degree (with honours) in English Language from the National University of Singapore and a master's degree in training from Leicester University. He is married with two sons.

Kevin SCULLY is Executive Chairman and Founder of NRA Capital. Kevin is an economist by training, has an honours degree in economics and spent the first two years of his working life in the regional and economics division of the Ministry of Foreign Affairs. He moved to equity research in the early 1980s and was in Schroder Securities for 12 years, where he progressed from being an analyst to Head of Research for Singapore/Malaysia in 1989, and to Managing Director for Singapore from 1995. He was also Head of Research at Kay Hian and HSBC Securities before starting NRA Capital in 1999.

Debra SOON is the Chief Editor of its TV News and Current Affairs Division. As Chief Editor, Ms Soon oversees the strategic development, positioning and editorial content of news and current affairs programmes for its English, Malay and Tamil Divisions. This includes coverage for regional network, Channel NewsAsia and other MediaCorp TV platforms such as Channel 5, Suria and Vasantham Central. Ms Soon has 15 years of experience in the media and communications industry. She started in broadcast journalism with the then Singapore Broadcasting Corporation and has also written for print. Her range of experience includes reporting on 'live' events in Singapore and from overseas, 'live' talk shows, leading general elections coverage and being Editor and presenter of the programme *In Parliament*. She served as President-elect SR Nathan's Press Secretary during the August 2005 Presidential Elections. Ms Soon is currently also a member of the National Council on Problem Gambling, and Chairperson of the Youth Sub-Committee and is a Council member of the Singapore Institute of International Affairs. Ms Soon obtained her Bachelor of Science in Economics and Master of Science degree in International Relations from the London School of Economics and Political Science under scholarship from the Singapore Broadcasting Corporation, and later the Television Corporation of Singapore. She is married to Cassius Cheong and they have two children.

TAN Chin Nam has had 33 years of distinguished service in the Singapore Civil Service holding various key appointments including Permanent Secretary, Ministry of Information, Communications and the Arts and Ministry of Manpower; Chairman, National Library Board; Chief Executive, Singapore Tourism Board; Managing Director, Economic Development Board; Chairman and General Manager, National Computer Board and Director, Systems and Computer Organisation, Ministry of Defence. He is now a senior corporate adviser serving on various boards. Apart from being Chairman of the Media Development Authority of Singapore, he is also Chairman, Temasek Management Services; Senior Adviser to the Salim Group; Non-Executive Independent Director of Stamford Land Ltd, Yeo Hiap Seng Ltd, PSA International Board and Raffles Education Corporation Ltd; Singapore's Governor of the Asia-Europe Foundation and Member of the Board of Trustees for the Bankinter Foundation for Innovation. He graduated from the University of Newcastle, Australia and the University of Bradford, UK and holds two Honorary Doctorates as well.

TAN Ern Ser is Associate Professor, Department of Sociology; Academic Convener, Singapore Studies Programme, Faculty of Arts and Social Sciences; and Vice-Dean of Students at the National University of Singapore. He is Principal Investigator of the World Values Survey (WVS) - Singapore and Asian Barometer - Singapore. He is also Principal Consultant for the National Orientations of Singaporeans (NOS) project series. Dr Tan is a member of the Economic and Social Research Network, the HDB Research Advisory Panel, and the Family Research Network. He has served as survey consultant to the Ministry of Community Development, Youth and Sports; the Ministry of Information, Communication and the Arts; the Ministry of Education, the Housing Development Board, REACH, and IPS. He was a member of the Sub-Committee on "Dealing with the Impact of Economic Restructuring", Economic Review Committee. Dr Tan has written on industrial relations, welfare policy, ethnic relations, social stratification, and political values. He is author of *Does Class Matter? Social Stratification and Orientations in Singapore* (2004). Dr Tan received his Doctor of Philosophy degree in Sociology from Cornell University.

TAN Kim Song is Practice Associate Professor of Economics, School of Economics at the Singapore Management University. Prior to this appointment, Dr Tan was the Managing Director of Fleet Boston Financial, Asia. He had also worked in Chase Manhattan Asia and Peregrine Fixed Income Ltd. Dr Tan has also worked at *The Straits Times*. Over the years, he has consulted widely in the region, especially in China and Indo-China. A Colombo Plan Scholar, Dr Tan received his Bachelor's degree in Economics with First Class Honours from Adelaide University. He received his Doctor of Philosophy degree from Yale University under a Yale Fellowship.

TAN Tarn How is a Senior Research Fellow at the Institute of Policy Studies. His research areas are in arts and cultural policy and media and Internet policy. He has written on the development of the arts in Singapore, in particular, fostering partnerships between the people, private and public sectors, on the creative industries in Singapore, China and Korea, on the history of cultural policy in Singapore, on censorship, and on the management of media in Singapore. He has also carried out research on the impact of the Internet and new technology on society, the regulation of the Internet, the role of new media in the 2008 Malaysian election and the 2006 Singapore election, and the impact of new media on old media. He was a journalist for nearly one and half decades before joining IPS. He has also been a teacher and television scriptwriter and is an award-winning playwright. He graduated from Cambridge University.

Norman VASU is the Coordinator of the Social Resilience Programme at the S. Rajaratnam School of International Studies (RSIS), Nanyang Technological University, Singapore. Dr Vasu specialises in the study of multiculturalism, identity-based conflict, transnational communities, cultural theory and political philosophy. Dr Vasu received his doctorate in International Politics from the University of Wales at Aberystwyth. He also holds a Master of Science degree in International Relations from the London School of Economics and a Master of Arts from the University of Glasgow. He has been a tutor at the Department of International Politics at the University of Wales Aberystwyth. At the same University, he had also been a lecturer on International Relations for the Centre of Widening Participation. He recently published a book titled *How Diasporic Peoples Maintain Their Identity in Multicultural Societies: Chinese, Africans and Jews*, and edited *Social Resilience in Singapore: Reflections from the London Bombings*.

Eleanor WONG joined the National University of Singapore in 2002 as Director of the Legal Skills Programme. Eleanor started her career with the Commercial Affairs Department, prosecuting complex commercial and securities frauds. She obtained a Masters in Corporate Law from New York University in 1990 and practiced in the New York office of Coudert Brothers, returning to Singapore in 1992. Eleanor specialised in regional banking and finance work for Coudert and, later, Orrick, Herrington & Sutcliffe. In 2000, she joined leading local television production company The Right Angle. There, she provided communications consultancy and training for top executives, and held several top management portfolios, including Chief Operating Officer and Chief Strategist. Eleanor is a published playwright, whose works have been produced in Singapore and ASEAN. Her most recent full-length work was titled *The Campaign to Confer the Public Service Star on JBJ*. A sometime television host, she anchored the critically well-received current affairs show *After Hours*. She was a member of the Remaking Singapore Committee and currently chairs the volunteer Council of the Singapore Advertising Standards Authority.

About the Institute of Policy Studies

The Institute of Policy Studies (IPS) was established in 1988 as a think-tank dedicated to fostering good governance in Singapore through strategic policy research and discussion. An autonomous research centre in the Lee Kuan Yew School of Public Policy at the National University of Singapore, IPS focuses on domestic developments in Singapore and on external relations. It employs a multi-disciplinary approach in its analysis with an emphasis on long-term strategic thinking.